BREAD MACHINE COOKBOOK

THE ESSENTIAL BREAD MAKING GUIDE
WITH 200 QUICK AND TASTY RECIPES FOR BEGINNERS
INCLUDING GLUTEN AND DAIRY FREE BREAD PREPARATIONS
AND VEGAN ALTERNATIVES

KANDICE LAWSON

TABLE OF CONTENTS

INTRODUCTION

A bread machine is a machine you use to bake bread, and you can buy it from any store for a very small amount of money. You can bake bread to add your favorite ingredients, such as herbs, cheese, and raisins. You prepare the dough in the bread machine using cups, and you can also use it as a cooking machine as it contains a steamer.

A bread machine is very simple to use. You just have to put all the ingredients in it and then press the start button. The only thing that could be a problem is when you first set it up as a timer. It will take minutes to set it up, and it is the machine that guides you all the way along, like a normal oven. A bread machine creates the most delicious bread. Nothing beats it as it mixes all the ingredients very well.

It must be very interesting to know how bread was first invented. At first, bread was baked in the ground. It was the Egyptians who first made excellent baking. It is assumed that they made the first bread that was ever baked, and it was just like a sticky dough that they baked. They had an unfair means of analysis when it came to baking.

The Romans were the first to introduce baths, roads, and weaving, and they also invented roads, bathing, and baking. The baking they invented was introduced in Rome. They added salt and sugar to the dough, and they used a few different types of loaves. The bread was good in quality, and they were very popular, so the Romans started baking a lot of them, and they sold them in the streets.

They added some herbs to the bread that were very healthy and tasty, and this is how the first bread was made, and they slowly became popular all over the world. The Egyptians also did the same, and they called the loaves 'barley loaves,' and they made them from barley. During the Roman Empire, bread was very popular, and the Romans loved it very much. They even used bread to replace the money.

The Romans' biggest contribution to baking was their creation of the coiled bread, and it is why bread now looks like that. The Romans named the bread after the people they were given to, and the bread was customized according to the people they were given to. It is believed that Christ brought some of his followers to Rome. It is said that a few years later, they were gone, and they were never heard or seen again. It is thought that they were sent to live in Persia, or they were sent to Babylon. For around 2 000 years, the ancient Persians had a very similar way of baking bread as the Romans did in ancient times.

They used many of the same means and techniques to bake their bread. The Europeans started a trend of baking their bread in molds. It is also believed that on the first day of training, bread was referred to as 'garli' bread because it had the same smell as garlic.

Many breads are well-known, such as wheat bread, white bread, cake bread, sandwich bread, etc. Before bread machines came out, it was much more difficult to bake any kind of bread, so all those breads had very little popularity. Now that we have bread machines, it has become very easy to bake those kinds of bread, and you can vary the amount of the ingredients at your will so you will make perfect bread that tastes great.

CHAPTER 1
Bread Machine

CHOOSING THE RIGHT BREAD MACHINE

A bread machine is a really good buy for your kitchen and will help you a lot. It will help you in baking bread, cakes, and even cookie dough. It comprises a mixing paddle, kneading blade, a baking chamber, and a cycling motor. The appliance comes with different modes and settings such as defrost, rise, bake, and timer. It provides you hassle-free batter kneading and baking, and you can set the timer for baking the bread. It helps you to bake bread quickly. Below are the factors you should take into consideration before buying a bread machine for yourself:

1.   The Baking Time

The baking time includes the rise time, kneading time, and baking time. The cycle will end by announcing the sound or beep. Some of the models are programmed so that the timer will proceed after the end of the baking time. When choosing a bread machine, look at the bake time and the time remaining in the cycle.

2.   The make-up of the Bread

Before buying a bread machine, look at the make-up of a good bread machine. Look at the quality of the bread. Does it matter to you that much? Is there any make-up issue with the bread? Does the bread appear to be great or mediocre? Does it look stale after the time? It would affect the overall taste of good bread.

3. Kneading Quality

If you will buy a bread machine and don't know how to knead the bread well, look for a higher quality kneading blade model. These blades have metal blades, which are made stronger than the blades found in many other appliances. These blades are tubular and longer and are precise. It would help you in kneading to the quality of the bread.

4. The Settings

Look at the settings on the product and how the appliance deals with different settings. A good bread machine should have a setting for the amount of dough. The settings should be varied to bake the bread for a small family or a large one. Verify that the parameters are stable and that the product is functioning correctly.

These things will help you in selecting a good bread machine.

MACHINE CYCLES AND SETTINGS

A bread machine can be a great option for those who want less hand mixing of the bread as it combines the ingredients, kneads, and rises in one simple step. Bread machine cycles are generally well-suited to recipes for bread made with few additional ingredients. Their ability to hold many ingredients and execute yeast recipes without hand-kneading results in little or no mess and little time spent kneading. Making loaves the old-fashioned way, by hand, could never be easier with these bread machine cycles. Here is a look at some of these cycles and settings:

1. Sourdough Cycle

You can make a loaf with sourdough starter and flour and water—the staple of American-style sourdoughs and Danish doughs. It is referred to as the "Sourdough cycle," and you won't need any other ingredients.

2. Whole Wheat

This cycle is ideal for those who want the taste of whole-grain bread without the high-fiber taste. Next to the basic white cycle, it produces the best whole-grain loaf. It is also great for those with a wheat allergy or gluten intolerance. This cycle mixes the dough well and can accommodate more of the natural bitterness of wheat.

3. French

It is great for making French bread, which tends to need longer to knead. The French cycle will do exactly this and also produce a delicious crust.

4. Sweet Bread

This cycle is intended for bread with a higher fat or sugar content or recipes that call for eggs or cheese. This cycle kneads for making sweet bread, such as cinnamon rolls and Danish pastries.

5. Fruit and Nut

You can use this cycle for cooking bread from dried fruit, nuts, and fruits.

6. Basic

The Basic cycle is also known as the "Quickbread cycle" for the recipe's simplicity.

7. Gluten-Free

The Gluten-Free cycle kneads dough for bread that tastes like traditional wheat bread but also contains no gluten. It also kneads well for bread made without eggs.

8. No-knead

As the name suggests, this is a quick option to produce loaves with a very open crumb, a nice crispy crust, and a balanced flavor. These loaves can be made in a bread machine using a one-pound, large or medium size.

PROCESS IN BREAD MACHINE

1. Put the Ingredients in the Bread Machine in the Order Indicated by the Manufacturer

The instruction manual will identify the order, kind, and amount of each ingredient. The liquids are added first, and then the powdered ingredients are added last. Adding ingredients is crucial, as it is the order in which the bread machine mixes the ingredients.

The user should add cold water or milk last, as the liquid expands when added with the soups.

2. Select Basic/White cycle

If the bread machine has both Basic/White and Basic/Whole Wheat cycles, select Basic/White cycle. Do not select the Medium/Dark cycle. Do not select Fast cycle. Do not make substitutions. Do not make changes. Always read instructions. Do not attempt the recipe without first obtaining a copy of the instructions or recipe.

3. Rising

The rising stage is an important step, as the yeast needs enough time to form air bubbles that cause carbon dioxide. It is what causes the bread to rise. If the yeast is not given enough rising time, the bread will be flat and dense.

The clock can be set according to the rising time required for the bread.

4.   Shaping the Loaf

The user can select to make one large loaf or two small loaves. When the bread loaves are placed on the baking pan, the cover is shut, and the buttons are pushed.

5.   Bake

When the rising period is over, the bread machine will start baking the bread. The baking process continues until the bread loaves are golden brown—this usually takes about an hour.

6.   The bread is taken out of the bread maker by the user with oven mitts and placed on a rack to cool. Enjoy the bread!

CHAPTER 2
Bread Ingredients

Below is the list of key ingredients you'll need to make bread and tips for selecting them.

FLOUR

Flour is the main ingredient for making bread. The standard recipe in this book uses bread flour. However, other types of flour can also be used in preparing bread, such as rye, whole wheat, oats, soy, and many more options of various flours. Please note that bread flour or white bread flour contains the most gluten and will result in more dense bread. On the other hand, some types of flour like cornflour or rice flour contain no gluten. So, if you want to get a decent rise of bread, add a small amount of white bread flour.

Important note: Before placing the flour in the bread machine, the flour must be sieved. Sifted flour is saturated with oxygen, which contributes to a better reaction with yeast. Thus, bread from sifted flour rises better and faster. It turns out more magnificent. Accordingly, for each recipe within this book, flour is measured in cups and aims for accuracy by including oz and grams. Keep in mind that first flour is measured and then sifted into your bread machine.

YEAST

Yeast has a crucial role in the bread-making process. It's the key ingredient to make the dough rise well and result in a smooth, pliable dough. The best yeast suggested for bread machines is bread machine yeast. You can also opt to use active dry yeast.

LIQUIDS

The liquid is vital in making bread since it activates the yeast and blends with flour to make a more elastic dough. Water may be the most common liquid used in making bread. However, to enhance the texture or flavor, some other liquid ingredients like milk, buttermilk, juice, or cream can also make bread.

Important Note: Closely pay attention to the temperature of the liquid to verify that it's warm. If the liquid is too cool, it'll stop the yeast action. If it's too hot, the liquid will destroy the yeast.

SWEETENER

Sugar is the common sweetener used for making bread, although other sweeteners like molasses, honey, jams, maple syrup, corn syrup, or brown sugar are also fine. Sugar is food for the yeast. However, giving too much sugar can inhibit gluten production. Unless you're going to add more gluten to the recipe—in the form of gluten flour, it's recommended to use two tbsps. of sugar for every cup of flour. Besides its yeast role, sugar also offers a sweet flavor to the bread, browns the bread, and tenderizes it.

SALT

Salt slows the rising time of the bread and gives the dough more time to develop the flavor. For the best result, it's highly suggested not to omit salt for any yeast bread recipes.

EGGS

Eggs are a leavening agent that helps the dough to rise well. Besides, eggs enhance the protein content, flavor, and overall color of the bread. Also, the eggs make the bread crust tenderer.

Please note that eggs should become room temperature before adding them to the dough process. Remove from fridge 1 hour before beginning.

FATS

Fat, which is involved in the bread-making process, will inhibit the gluten and prevent it from rising as high as the bread without any fats. The good part about fats—especially olive oil and butter-enriches the flavor, tenderizes the texture, and extends the bread's life.

The ingredients listed above are only the basics for making bread. You can always follow your creativity by adding some herbs and spices to enhance the bread's taste and appearance. All you have to pay attention to is that the crucial step in making bread using a bread machine is measuring the ingredients accurately. It's preferable to use a digital scale, liquid measuring cups, dry measuring cups, and measuring spoons with an accurate number for maximum accuracy.

CHAPTER 3
Types Of Flour

Flour is the most important ingredient in the baking process. Using bad flour will give you a bad-tasting bread, and a good one will leave you wanting more. Apart from the nutrition and health benefit of different flours that can be used, another main aspect of choosing flour revolves around the amount of gluten it contains. It is a chemical that is made by two types of protein—glutenin and gliadin. Together they determine the elasticity, the firmness, and the resistance to tear in a dough. It is the chemical that makes bread possible by flour.

There are four most commonly used flours for making bread all over the world. These are:

1. ALL-PURPOSE FLOUR

Most people around the world utilize this type of flour for their homemade bread. It has a high gluten content, up to 11%, and is made by combining two types of wheat—soft and hard wheat. These are available in two forms in the market.

Unbleached all-purpose flour is aged naturally without the use of any chemicals. Over time, the flour oxides and loses its yellowish pigment. This kind of flour retains the nutrient value and has a higher level of vitamins and minerals

Bleached all-purpose flour is aged quickly by exposing it to a chemical called chlorine dioxide. The flour loses its yellowish pigment and is ready to be sold to the world. It has been shown that the chemical process affects the gluten content of the flour. It losses many of its nutrients in this destructive process, so the nutrients are added again to match its unbleached counterpart. These nutrients are known as fortified nutrients, and you see them mentioned on the packaging.

There is not much difference in either the flour in taste or baking process, although some people prefer using the unbleached kind for making bread rather than the bleached ones. This flour is best for making white bread.

2. BREAD FLOUR

This flour is manufactured only for the sole purpose of making the best quality bread. It is used in commercially distributed bread because it gives the best texture and holds up nicely. It also is available in two forms in the market. This bread has a much higher gluten content than all-purpose flour, ranging from 11% to 14%.

Unbleached bread flour is also aged naturally, and no chemicals are used. It is made up of hard red spring wheat and is sold at a much heftier price.

Bleached bread flour is aged quickly and, like all-purpose flour, loses many of its nutrients along the way. Those nutrients are added again as fortified nutrients, and then it is sold at a lower price.

Because of the higher amount of gluten in this flour, you will need to use a lot more water to form the dough. You can get used to the ratio after making a few pieces of bread using this flour.

3. WHOLE-WHEAT FLOUR

This flour comes from the whole wheat berry and is not stripped of its bran and germ. 100% whole wheat flour contains no additives or preservatives, and no chemical process has been done that will take away any nutrients. The flour is the most natural flour present on the market shelves.

The gluten content is very high in this flour, almost reaching up to 16%. It is the highest gluten percentage a flour can have. Now, why isn't this flour then used all around the world to make the fluffiest bread? Whole wheat is a lot denser than other flours because it is not finely ground. The hulls present within it interfere with the gluten strands. This way, the gluten becomes less noticeable than its high percentage would suggest.

The flavor of all-natural grains with all its structures attached gives a nutty flavor and different textures. The texture can be soft or coarse and baked into delicious, chewy bread. It is the ideal flour used to make brown bread. However, brown bread can be made with any whole grain like rye, etc.

4. WHITE WHOLE WHEAT FLOUR

White whole wheat flour comes from white spring wheat. It provides the nutritional benefits of whole wheat but has a milder and lighter taste to it. Its gluten percentage is about 12%, so it can be a good replacement for all-purpose flour. The grain it is made out of is lighter in color and sweet in taste. The bread also leaves a sweet aftertaste because of it.

CHAPTER 4
Types Of Yeast

Yeasts are defined as all substances that contribute to the increase in a dough's volume following fermentation.

1. BEER YEAST

This type of yeast is generally used for home baking, obtained from beer fermentation residues. In contrast, today, it is obtained from molasses, a by-product of beet and sugar cane processing, and compressed and marketed in 25-gram cakes for home baking and 500-gram cakes for professional baking. When reference is made in the recipes to 'panett,' the 25-gram bread is implied. Beware, however, that this is not a law!

The brewer's yeast can also be dry in granules, in sachets generally dosed for 500 grams of flour.

2. NATURAL YEAST OR MOTHER YEAST

Ideal for making some types of bread (homemade, regional bread) and some bread cakes (panettone, doves, etc.), it is obtained by prolonged fermentation of a dough of flour, water, even with the addition of some agents that promote fermentation such as yogurt, raw honey or very ripe fruit. The fermented dough is usually subjected to a phase of refreshments and washing according to the various recipes.

Paste "di Riport."

They provide the dough with a charge of already active yeasts that allow a faster fermentation and give it digestibility and a crunchy and crumbly crust. Preserved in the refrigerator, covered or oiled on the surface to prevent crust formation, they maintain their fermentative qualities for no longer than a week.

THE CHARIOT

It is prepared several hours before the final dough, kneading flour with water and a small amount of brewer's yeast (e.g., 350 g white flour, 5 g brewer's yeast) to obtain a very soft dough. If prepared more than 24 hours in advance, the chariot must be reworked and refreshed with more flour and water to keep the yeast alive and active.

THE RISING

It is the method most often indicated in the recipes as it offers good results even to the less expert in the field. With a certain advance that can vary from 2-3 hours up to 8 hours, a fairly soft batter is prepared, using the same amount of flour and water with the addition of a small amount of yeast.

INDIRECT DOUGH AND LEAVENING

There are two basic methods for preparing leavened products (bread and cakes). The first, most used, is to put all the ingredients at the same time (liquids, flours, yeast, fats, sugars, etc.) on the pastry board, in a bowl or the basket of the bread machine, making the dough and leavening and then baking the product. This system takes the technical name of "Direct dough." It has the advantage of being the fastest system to make a leavened product; on the other hand, you have to use fairly high doses of beer yeast, of which we will find the taste in a more or less decisive way in the finished product. The other method is called "Impasto Indiretto" (Indirect dough), which involves using smaller brewer's yeast quantities and consists of two main phases. The first phase involves a dough of only water, flour, and yeast, with the possible addition of sugar as other food for the yeast, a leavening time of the first dough more or less long, and then the addition of all the other ingredients (liquids, flours, "any other yeas," fats, sugars, etc.) for the realization of the finished product. During the first dough, there will be a reproduction/propagation of the yeast very similar to what happens with yogurt ferments; as in the latter case, where a certain amount of milk, under particular conditions and after the addition of a small percentage of yogurt is completely transformed into yogurt, so, for the water and flour dough with the addition of a certain amount of yeast, depending on the percentage of yeast used and the time that will be allowed for the yeast to reproduce, we will have the transformation of the entire first dough into a leavening mass. This procedure, although longer and more laborious, allows us to obtain a considerable leavening strength using only small quantities of yeast, which will allow us to taste products with a more pleasant taste, a lower yeast flavor, better organoleptic characteristics, and in some cases, the better shelf life of the finished product.

We could classify some subcategories according to the percentage of brewer's yeast used and the yeast-fermentation times used in indirect mixes. —The first, the fastest, is called "yeas," a soft dough where the amount of yeast can be similar to that used for the direct dough, and the time required is established by eye when the dough has doubled its initial volume. If we increase the leavening time to about 10 hours at this first indirect dough, we will obtain the "botto." - By further increasing the leavening time up to the 24-hour threshold, we will obtain the "big" —Last but not least: the "poolis," a dough where the parts of flour and water are equal and where the percentage of yeast, compared to flour, changes according to the leavening/fermentation time that we decide to adopt. The ideal room temperature for leavening is around 20–23°C as you should always use warm water for the dough. The ideal flour is strong. The dough must be quite short. —For a leavening time of 2 hours, the percentage of yeast should be about 3% of the flour's weight. —For a rising time of 3 hours, the percentage of yeast should be about 1.5% of the flour's weight. —For a 12-hour leavening time, the percentage of yeast should be about 0.5% of the flour's weight. —For a 16-hour rise, the percentage of yeast should be about 0.1% of the flour's weight.

CHAPTER 5
Classic Bread Recipes

1. CLASSIC WHITE BREAD

PREPARATION: 10 MIN | **COOKING:** 2-4 H | **SERVES:** 12

INGREDIENTS

- 1 cup boiling water (110 ° F/45 ° C).
- 3 tablespoons white sugar
- 1 1/2 teaspoons salt
- 3 tablespoons vegetable oil
- 3 cups bread flour
- 2 1/4 teaspoons dry yeast

DIRECTIONS

1. Place sugar, water, oil, salt, bread flour, and yeast in bread machine pan.
2. Bake on the setting of White Bread. Before slicing, cool on wire racks.

Nutritions *(Per serving):*

Calories: 121 kcal
Protein: 5.44 g

Fat: 1.1 g
Carbohydrates: 22.39 g

2. FLUFFY WHITE BREAD

PREPARATION: 15 MIN   **COOKING:** 30 MIN   **SERVES:** 12

INGREDIENTS

- 1 cup warm water
- 2 Tbsp white sugar
- 2.25 Tsp ferment/yeast
- 3 cups bread flour
- 1/4 Melted Butter
- 1 teaspoon salt

DIRECTIONS

1. Having your bread machine prepared to go (or your mixing pot, or whichever form you choose), put in the machine warm water (set aside 2 tbsp), sugar, and yeast. Offer a blend to help dissolve easily. Let it get sparkling and bubbly, approximately 10 minutes.
2. Tangzhongin, while your yeast gets revved up, start the tangzhong while using 3 tbsp flour and 2 tbsp water in a pot and warm at low heat until a nice gooey roux is obtained. This will only take about two minutes.
3. Tangzhong starter, butter, salt, flour goes (in order) into your bread machine.
4. Set "dough" on the bread machine, and walk away.
5. Upon completion of the dough cycle, remove the dough over to a floured surface, break it down in half, and punch.
6. Place the dough in two loaf pans.
7. Preheat the oven to 350 as the batter is raised a second time.
8. Place an ovenproof jar inside the oven with around 2 cups of water. The water would produce steam and keep you from having a rough, hard crust.
9. Put your loaf pans in the oven once the oven is ready and bake for 30 minutes.
10. This bread must be stored in a zip-top bag for around a week and stay soft and ready to eat.

Nutritions *(Per serving):*

Calories: 124 kcal
Protein: 5.30 g

Fat: 1.2 g
Carbohydrates: 22.26 g

3. CLASSIC FRENCH BREAD

PREPARATION: 10 MIN   **COOKING:** 1 H 30 MIN   **SERVES:** 14

INGREDIENTS

- 3 1/2 cups bread flour
- 1 teaspoon salt
- 1 (1/4 ounce) active dry yeast
- 1 1/4teaspoon warm water

DIRECTIONS

1. Place ingredients according to the manufacturer's instructions in the bread machine.
2. Start the machine after setting the dough.
3. Remove the dough with greased hands and slice it in half on a floured surface when the dough process is over.
4. Take every half of the dough and roll in French bread form to make a bread roll about 12 inches long.
5. Place on the baking sheet and seal with a towel.
6. Let it rise, about 1 hour until it doubles.
7. Preheat the oven to 450 ° C.
8. Bake for 20 to 25 minutes on each side; while baking, turn to pan around once in the midpoint.
9. Remove the baked loaves and cool them to wire racks.

Nutritions *(Per serving):*

Calories: 163 kcal
Protein: 6.63 g

Fat: 1.09 g
Carbohydrates: 31.58 g

4. GOLDEN WHEAT BREAD

PREPARATION: 10 MIN   **COOKING:** 2-4 H   **SERVES:** 14

INGREDIENTS

- One cup plus 2 tablespoons water (70 to 80 °)
- One-quarter cup canola oil
- Two tablespoons mustard
- 2 tablespoons honey
- 1 Teaspoon oil
- 2-1/2 cups flour in bread
- 1 Cup whole wheat flour
- 2-1/4 tsp dry yeast

DIRECTIONS

1. Place ingredients in bread machine pan in the order proposed by the manufacturer. Select the basic setting for the bread. Choose the color of the crust and the size of the bread, if available.
2. Bake according to the bread machine's directions (check the dough after 5 minutes of blending; add 1-2 spoons of flour or water if required).

Nutritions *(Per serving):*

Calories: 136 kcal
Protein: 5.47 g

Fat: 1.65 g
Carbohydrates: 24.83 g

5. WHOLE WHEAT BREAD

PREPARATION: 10 MIN | **COOKING:** 2-4 H | **SERVES:** 14

INGREDIENTS

- 1 1/4 cups hot water
- 2 Tbsp. of olive oil
- 1/4 cup maple syrup (or honey liquid)
- 3 1/2 cup wheat flour
- 1 1/2teaspoons salt
- 2 Instant yeast Teaspoons

DIRECTIONS

1. In the order suggested, add all ingredients to the bread machine.
2. If your bread maker has one, then choose the "whole wheat" setting. If not, choose white simple.
3. Before cutting, enable the bread to cool properly.

Nutritions *(Per serving):*

Calories: 129 kcal
Protein: 6.35 g

Fat: 1.79 g
Carbohydrates: 21.78 g

6. BREAD MACHINE NAAN

PREPARATION: 10 MIN   **COOKING:** 1-3 H   **SERVES:** 16

INGREDIENTS

- 2% hot 3/4 cup milk (70 ° to 80 °)
- 3/4 Cup Basic Yogurt
- 1 large egg, beaten at room temperature
- 2 tbsp canola oil
- 2 tsp sugar
- 1 teaspoon salt
- 1 teaspoon baking powder
- 4 Cups Flour Bread
- 2 teaspoons active dry yeast

DIRECTIONS

1. Put all ingredients in the bread maker pan in the order suggested by the company. Choose dough setting (check the dough after mixing for 5 minutes; add 1 to 2 spoonfuls of flour if required).
2. Turn the dough onto a floured surface when the cycle is complete. Divide into six parts: mold into balls. Roll every single ball into a 1/4-in. Dense oval. Let them rest for five minutes.
3. Brush water to the tops. Cover and cook dough in a large buttered skillet, soggy end down, over medium-high temperature for 1 minute. Move dough; cover and cook for more than 30 seconds, or until golden brown. Continue for remaining dough.

Nutritions *(Per serving):*

Calories: 146 kcal
Protein: 5.2 g

Fat: 3.42 g
Carbohydrates: 23.57 g

7. PUMPKIN SPICE QUICK BREAD

PREPARATION: 10 MIN   **COOKING:** 1-3 H   **SERVES:** 6

INGREDIENTS

- One cup sugar
- 1 Cup packaged pumpkin
- One-third cup vegetable oil
- 1 Vanilla Teaspoon
- 2 Eggs
- 1 1/2 cups All-purpose Gold Medal meal or Better for Bread meal
- Baking powder 2 teaspoons
- 1/4 tsp salt
- 1 tsp cinnamon
- Nutmeg ground 1/4 teaspoon
- Ground cloves 1/8 teaspoon
- Sliced nuts 1/2 cup, if necessary

DIRECTIONS

1. Grease bread machine pans generously and kneading blade too.
2. In the order suggested by the manufacturer, measure carefully to put all ingredients in the bread machine pan.
3. Simply select the Quick Bread cycle. Open the lid after 3 minutes into the cycle and scrape the sides of the pan carefully. Close your lid to continue cycling.
4. Cool bread for 10 minutes. Shift it from pan to wire rack or follow suggestions from the manufacturer.

Nutritions *(Per serving):*

Calories: 153 kcal
Protein: 2.47 g

Fat: 6.33 g
Carbohydrates: 21.97 g

8. MULTIGRAIN BREAD

PREPARATION: 10 MIN   **COOKING:** 1-4 H   **SERVES:** 12

INGREDIENTS

- Water 1-1/3 cups (70 °-80 °)
- 2 spoon shortenings
- 2 tablespoons honey
- 1/2 cup 7-grain cereal
- 1/3 cup flax seed
- 2 Tablespoons non-fat powdered dry milk
- 2 Tablespoons sunflower kernels not salted
- 1 Spoonful of sesame seeds
- 1 teaspoon salt
- 2 cups all-purpose flour
- 1 Cup the whole wheat flour
- 1 pack (1/4 ounce) of active dry yeast

DIRECTIONS

1. Put all the ingredients in the bread mold in the order recommended by the manufacturer.
2. Select the basic setting for the bread. Pick the color of the crust and size of the loaf, if appropriate.
3. Bake according to the bread machine's directions (check the dough after five minutes of melding; add 1 to 2 spoons of water or flour if necessary).

Nutritions *(Per serving):*

Calories: 114 kcal
Protein: 5.31 g

Fat: 6.5 g
Carbohydrates: 8.62 g

9. RUSTIC ITALIAN BREAD

PREPARATION: 10 MIN	**COOKING:** 1 H	**SERVES:** 8

INGREDIENTS

- 1 1/2tbsp sugar
- 1 1/2tbsp rosemary
- 1 Tablespoon yeast
- Extra Rosemary (for topping up)
- Salt (to put on garnish)
- 3/4Cups water
- 2 Tbsp. of olive oil
- 2 cups Flour
- 1 tablespoon salt

DIRECTIONS

1. Place the ingredients into your bread machine, as per the manufacturer's instructions.
2. Set the machine to "dough cycle" and wait (on most machines, this will take about 1/2hours for a full cycle).
3. When the process has finished, separate the dough from the machine and put it on a lightly greased baking sheet.
4. Turn the dough by hand into a triangular mound, distributing it thinly, about an inch or two thick.
5. Cover the dough and let it sprout for almost an hour in a warm environment or till it has increased in size. (This is a great time to preheat ahead and turn the oven on).
6. Brush slightly with olive oil. Sprinkle with the rosemary and salt if you want.
7. Bake for about 20-25 minutes at 375 ° F, until golden and crispy.
8. Serve with fresh ground pepper seasoned with olive oil.

Nutritions *(Per serving):*

Calories: 138 kcal
Protein: 4.49 g

Fat: 1.79 g
Carbohydrates: 25.5 g

10. BREAD MACHINE CHALLAH

PREPARATION: 5 MIN | **COOKING:** 1-3 H | **SERVES:** 12

INGREDIENTS

- 3/4 cups milk
- 2 Eggs 2
- Margarine: 3 Tablespoons
- 3 cups flour for bread
- One-fourth cup white sugar
- 1 1/2teaspoons salt
- 1 1/2 tsp active dry yeast

DIRECTIONS

1. Within the manufacturer's suggested order, add ingredients to the bread machine pan.
2. Choose sweet Bread and Light Crust setup (or Simple if you don't have this option). Starting.

Nutritions *(Per serving):*

Calories: 119 kcal
Protein: 5.33 g

Fat: 1.08 g
Carbohydrates: 21.96 g

11. BREAD MACHINE BASIC BAGELS

PREPARATION: 10 MIN	**COOKING:** 2-4 H	**SERVES:** 12

INGREDIENTS

- 1 1/8 cup water, should be warm
- 3 cups white flour
- 3 1/3 tablespoons brown sugar
- 1 teaspoon salt
- 3 1/4 teaspoons dry yeast

DIRECTIONS

1. Insert ingredients into the bread machine as instructed by the maker. After the first knead, take away the dough from the machine for about 20 to 30 minutes.
2. Put dough on a surface that is floured. Split into 8 parts. Shape balls and gently press thumb into the ball center and gradually stretch into bagel form.
3. As bagels rise, put in a wide saucepan three-quarter of the water and a tablespoon of sugar to a fast boil. Drop 2-3 bagels into boiling water, using a skillet.
4. Boil 1/2minutes on each side. Remove and cool on a rack for 1 minute, brush with an egg, and sprinkle, if necessary, with sesame or poppy seed. Bake at 400 degrees F, sprinkled with cornmeal on a baking dish, until golden-around 15 minutes.

Nutritions *(Per serving):*

Calories: 147 kcal
Protein: 5.68 g

Fat: 0.88 g
Carbohydrates: 29.13 g

12. POTATO BREAD

PREPARATION: 10 MIN   **COOKING:** 2-4 H   **SERVES:** 12

INGREDIENTS

- Water: 1 + 1/4 cup
- Vegetable oil 3 TBSP
- 3 cups flour
- 3 Tbsp sugar
- 1 + 1/2 tsp salt
- 1 Tsp lemon zest
- 1/2 tsp white pepper
- 2 Tsp Dry chopped onions
- 1/2Cup Flacks of Potato
- 2 + 1/4 tsp dry, active yeast

DIRECTIONS

1. Add the additives in the order indicated in the pan. Use Cycle of Basic or White Bread and Medium / Normal Crust.
2. After kneading for 5 minutes, test the texture of the flour. The dough will be in a cheesy ball of softness. Add water, 1/2to 1 tablespoon at a time if it is dry and steep. If it is too soggy and stringy, add 1 cubic meter of flour at a time.
3. Active Dry Yeast can be replaced by Instant (fast-rising) in your recipes instead. Just assume your dough to rise quickly when using Instant Yeast. Still, let the dough increase until it is ready. When baking using traditional methods, use similar quantities. Using 1/2tsp Instant Yeast OR 3/4tsp Active Dried Yeast per cup flour in your compost while using the Bread Machine.

Nutritions *(Per serving):*

Calories: 136 kcal
Protein: 6.38 g

Fat: 1.6 g
Carbohydrates: 24.01 g

13. A BAKERS SECRET FOR BREAD MACHINES

PREPARATION: 5 MIN | **COOKING:** 2 H 55 MIN | **SERVES:** 10

INGREDIENTS

- 7 fluid ounces of warm water (110 degrees F/45 degrees C)
- 2 tablespoons lard
- 1 (.25 ounce) package of active dry yeast
- 2 3/4 cups bread flour
- 1 teaspoon salt
- 1 teaspoon ground cinnamon (optional)

DIRECTIONS

1. Ignore the bread machine directions. Place warm water and lard into the bread machine pan. Sprinkle in the yeast. Pour in flour and salt.
2. Toss in cinnamon if desired. Select cycle; press Start.

Nutritions *(Per serving):*

| Calories: 162 kcal | Cholesterol: 2 mg | Carbohydrates: | Protein: 4.8 g |
| Total Fat: 3.2 g | Sodium: 234 mg | 27.8 g | |

14. ALLIGATOR ANIMAL ITALIAN BREAD

PREPARATION: 30MIN   **COOKING:** 20 MIN   **SERVES:** 8

INGREDIENTS

For the dough:
- One cup warm water
- 3 cups all-purpose flour
- 1 tablespoon vital wheat gluten (optional)
- 1 1/2 teaspoons salt
- 2 1/2 teaspoons instant yeast

For decorating:
- 2 raisins
- 1 egg
- 1 tablespoon water

DIRECTIONS

1. Mix the water, flour, gluten (if using), salt, and yeast in your bread machine and mix using the machine's dough cycle. The dough should nicely pull away from the sides. Add flour or water as needed during the mixing process, not to end up too sticky or dry. At the end of the first ascending cycle, press in the dough and place it on a lightly floured surface.
2. Grease a baking sheet or cover it with parchment paper. Roll out the batter into a 3/4-inch square and divide into four pieces. Roll out three of the jelly-roll style pieces, and align them seam-side down on the baking sheet to form the head, body, and tail. The ends of the connected pieces must be slightly touched.
3. Grease your hands lightly and shape the dough like you're working with clay. Extend the tail until it is curved and slender, then lengthen the nose end.
4. Slice nose horizontally at the end to form alligator mouth; keep the mouth open with greased aluminum foil wedge.
5. From the remaining quarter of the dough, trim off a tiny piece to use for the eyes. Slice the remainder into four "log" for legs, flattening one end of each leg and inserting it under the alligator's body. Form the legs into slight folds when positioning them on the plate. Cut short slices on the other end of the leg for claws. Use scissors to snip shallow cuts over the dough's surface (this will form the alligator's spiky skin). Roll the reserved dough into small balls for the eyes, filling each with a raisin.
6. Preheat an oven to 400 degrees F. Beat the egg with one tablespoon of warm water in a bowl.
7. Let the alligator rise in a warm position until fully proofed, about 30 minutes (poke your index and middle fingers into the sides of the bread). The indentation should remain. Lightly brush the batter with the egg wash and bake it in the preheated oven until golden brown, about 20 minutes. Remove the alligator from the baking sheet with a spatula and transfer it to a wire rack. Remove the aluminum foil when cool.

Nutritions *(Per serving):*

Calories: 187 kcal   Cholesterol: 20 mg   Carbohydrates: Protein: 6.6 g
Total Fat: 1.1 g   Sodium: 446 mg   36.7 g

15. AMISH BREAD

PREPARATION: 5 MIN | **COOKING:** 3 H | **SERVES:** 12

INGREDIENTS

- 2 3/4 cups bread flour
- 1/4 cup canola oil
- 1 teaspoon active dry yeast
- 1/4 cup white sugar
- 1/2 teaspoon salt
- 18 tablespoons warm water

DIRECTIONS

1. Add the ingredients in the pan of the bread machine in the sequence recommended by the manufacturer. Select White Bread cycle; press Start.
2. When the dough has raised once and the second cycle of kneading begins, turn the machine off. Reset by pressing Start once again. It will give the dough two full raising cycles before the final raising cycle before baking.

Nutritions *(Per serving):*

Calories: 58 kcal
Total Fat: 4.7 g

Cholesterol: 0 mg
Sodium: 98 mg

Carbohydrates: 4.3 g

Protein: 0.1 g

16. APRICOT OAT BREAD

PREPARATION: 10 MIN **COOKING:** 30 MIN **SERVES:** 12

INGREDIENTS

- 4 1/4 cups bread flour
- 2/3 cup rolled oats
- 1 tablespoon white sugar
- 2 teaspoons active dry yeast
- 1 1/2 teaspoons salt
- 1 teaspoon ground cinnamon
- 2 tablespoons butter, cut up
- 1 2/3 cups orange juice
- 1/2 cup diced dried apricots
- 2 tablespoons honey, warmed

DIRECTIONS

1. Add bread ingredients in the pan of the bread machine in the sequence recommended by the manufacturer; add the dried apricots just before the kneading cycle ends.
2. Remove the bread quickly from the machine when it's finished, and glaze with the warmed honey. Allow to cool completely before serving.

Nutritions *(Per serving):*

Calories: 80 kcal
Total Fat: 2.3 g

Cholesterol: 5 mg
Sodium: 306 mg

Carbohydrates: 14.4 g

Protein: 1.3 g

17. BASIC WHITE BREAD

PREPARATION: 5 MIN	**COOKING:** 3H	**SERVES:** 12

INGREDIENTS

- 1 1/4 cups warm water
- 1 tablespoon butter, softened
- 1 tablespoon white sugar
- 1 teaspoon salt
- 3 cups bread flour
- 2 tablespoons dry milk powder
- 1 (.25 ounce) package active dry yeast

DIRECTIONS

1. Add ingredients in the pan of the bread machine in the sequence recommended by the manufacturer.
2. Select White Bread setting; press Start.

Nutritions *(Per serving):*

Calories: 142 kcal	Cholesterol: 3 mg	Carbohydrates: 26.7 g	Protein: 4.8 g
Total Fat: 1.6 g	Sodium: 209 mg		

18. BASIL AND SUNDRIED TOMATO BREAD

PREPARATION: 10 MIN   **COOKING:** 2-4 H   **SERVES:** 12

INGREDIENTS

- 2 1/4 teaspoons active dry yeast
- 3 cups bread flour
- 3 tablespoons wheat bran
- 1/3 cup quinoa
- 3 tablespoons instant powdered milk
- 1 tablespoon dried basil
- 1/3 cup chopped sun-dried tomatoes
- 1 teaspoon salt
- 1 1/4 cups water
- 1 cup boiling water to cover

DIRECTIONS

1. In a bowl, pour boiling water over sun-dried tomato halves to cover. Soak for 10 minutes, drain, and cool to room temperature. With scissors, snip into 1/4 inch pieces.
2. Place all ingredients into the pan of the bread machine in the order recommended by the manufacturer. Select the Basic or White Bread cycle, and Start.

Nutritions *(Per serving):*

Calories: 156 kcal
Total Fat: 1 g

Cholesterol: < 1 mg
Sodium: 204 mg

Carbohydrates: 30.6 g

Protein: 5.9 g

19. BAXIS WHITE BREAD

PREPARATION: 5 MIN   **COOKING:** 2 H 15 MIN   **SERVES:** 10

INGREDIENTS

- 1 1/2 teaspoons active dry yeast
- 2 cups bread flour
- 1 teaspoon salt
- 1 tablespoon white sugar
- 1 tablespoon dry milk powder
- 1 tablespoon butter, softened
- 3/4 cup water

DIRECTIONS

1. Add ingredients in the pan of the bread machine in the sequence recommended by the manufacturer.
2. Select Medium cycle; press Start. When done, remove bread from pan and let cool on a wire rack.

Nutritions *(Per serving):*

Calories: 19 kcal
Total Fat: 1.2 g

Cholesterol: 3 mg
Sodium: 245 mg

Total Carbohydrate: 1.9 g

Protein: 0.5 g

20. BEST BREAD MACHINE BREAD

PREPARATION: 10 MIN | **COOKING:** 40 MIN | **SERVES:** 12

INGREDIENTS

- 1 cup warm water
- 2 tablespoons white sugar
- 1 (.25 ounce) package bread machine yeast
- 1/4 cup vegetable oil
- 3 cups bread flour
- 1 teaspoon salt

DIRECTIONS

1. Stir in water, sugar, and yeast to the pan of the bread maker. Leave the yeast to dissolve and froth for 10 minutes.
2. Combine the oil, flour, and salt with the yeast. Select Basic or White Bread setting. Press Start.

Nutritions *(Per serving):*

Calories: 174 kcal	*Cholesterol: 0 mg*	*Carbohydrates: 27.1 g*	*Protein: 4.3 g*
Total Fat: 5.2 g	*Sodium: 195 mg*		

21. BUTTERMILK WHITE BREAD

PREPARATION: 5 MIN | **COOKING:** 3 H | **SERVES:** 12

INGREDIENTS

- 1 1/8 cups water
- 3 tablespoons honey
- 1 tablespoon margarine
- 1 1/2 teaspoons salt
- 3 cups bread flour
- 2 teaspoons active dry yeast
- 4 tablespoons powdered buttermilk

DIRECTIONS

1. Combine ingredients to bread machine pan in the sequence recommended by your manufacturer.
2. Use medium crust and white bread settings. Use less yeast during hot, humid summer months.

Nutritions *(Per serving):*

Calories: 34 calories
Total Fat: 1 g
Cholesterol: 1 mg

Sodium: 313 mg
Total Carbohydrate: 5.7 g

Protein: 1 g

22. CINNAMON SWIRL BREAD FOR THE BREAD MACHINE

PREPARATION: 1 H 35   **COOKING:** 30 MIN   **SERVES:** 24

INGREDIENTS

- 1 cup milk
- 2 eggs
- 1/4 cup butter
- 4 cups bread flour
- 1/4 cup white sugar
- 1 teaspoon salt
- 1 1/2 teaspoons (active dry yeast)
- 1/2 cup chopped walnuts
- 1/2 cup packed brown sugar
- 2 teaspoons ground cinnamon
- 2 tablespoons softened butter, divided
- 2 teaspoons sifted confectioners' sugar, divided (optional)

DIRECTIONS

1. Put the milk, eggs, 1/4 cup butter, bread flour, sugar, salt, and yeast into a bread maker in the sequence suggested by the manufacturer, select the dough setting and start the machine.
2. Once the dough cycle has ended, transfer the dough to a floured work surface and punch down. Let the dough rest for 10 minutes.
3. Combine walnuts, brown sugar, and cinnamon in a bowl.
4. Divide dough in half and roll each half into a rectangle about 9x14 inches. Spread 1 tablespoon of softened butter over each dough rectangle and evenly sprinkle dough with half the walnut mixture. Roll out the dough rectangles, beginning with the short ends, and pinch seams closed.
5. Grease 2 9x5-inch loaf pans. Fit the rolled loaves into the loaf pans with seam sides down. Cover and leave to rise until the size is almost doubled, about 30 minutes.
6. Warm oven to 350 degrees F (175 degrees C).
7. Bake loaves in the preheated oven until lightly golden brown, about 30 minutes. If loaves brown too quickly, lightly cover with aluminum foil for the last 10 minutes of baking. Let stand for 10 minutes before removing it to complete the cooling on the grids. Sprinkle the tops of each loaf with 1 teaspoon confectioners' sugar.

Nutritions *(Per serving):*

Calories: 80 kcal	Cholesterol: 24 mg	Carbohydrates: 7.9 g	Protein: 1.4 g
Total Fat: 5.1 g	Sodium: 129 mg		

23. GRANDMAS ENGLISH MUFFIN BREAD

PREPARATION: 15 MIN   **COOKING:** 15 MIN   **SERVES:** 24

INGREDIENTS

- 3 cups all-purpose flour
- 2 1/4 teaspoons active dry yeast
- 1/2 tablespoon white sugar
- 1 teaspoon salt
- 1/8 teaspoon baking powder
- 1 cup warm milk
- 1/4 cup water

DIRECTIONS

1. Combine ingredients in the bread machine pan in the sequence suggested by the manufacturer. Select the dough cycle.
2. Divide dough into two unequal parts, and shape into loaves. Place in one 9 x 5-inch loaf pan and one 7 x 3-inch loaf pan; non-stick pans are preferable but greased, and floured normal pans will suffice. Cover and let stand until the size doubles.
3. Bake at 400 degrees F (205 degrees C) for about 15 minutes. Grandma bakes hers longer for a more browned and chewier crust.

Nutritions *(Per serving):*

Calories: 64 kcal   Cholesterol: < 1 mg   Carbohydrates: Protein: 2.1 g
Total Fat: 0.4 g   Sodium: 104 mg   12.8 g

24. HOMEMADE WONDERFUL BREAD

PREPARATION: 10 MIN **COOKING:** 3 H **SERVES:** 15

INGREDIENTS

- 2 1/2 teaspoons active dry yeast
- 1/4 cup warm water
- 1 tablespoon white sugar
- 4 cups all-purpose flour
- 1/4 cup dry potato flakes
- 1/4 cup dry milk powder
- 2 teaspoons salt
- 1/4 cup white sugar
- 2 tablespoons margarine
- 1 cup warm water

DIRECTIONS

1. Whisk together the yeast, 1/4 cup warm water, and sugar. Allow to sit for 15 minutes.
2. Add ingredients in the sequence suggested by your manufacturer, including the yeast mixture. Select the basic and light crust setting.

Nutritions *(Per serving):*

Calories: 162 kcal
Total Fat: 1.8 g
Cholesterol: < 1 mg
Sodium: 339 mg
Carbohydrates: 31.6 g
Protein: 4.5 g

25. HONEY WHITE BREAD

PREPARATION: 5 MIN   **COOKING:** 1-3 H   **SERVES:** 12

INGREDIENTS

- 1 cup milk
- 3 tablespoons unsalted butter, melted
- 2 tablespoons honey
- 3 cups bread flour
- 3/4 teaspoon salt
- 3/4 teaspoon vitamin c powder
- 3/4 teaspoon ground ginger
- 1 1/2 teaspoons (active dry yeast)

DIRECTIONS

1. Put the ingredients together in the order suggested in your bread maker manual.
2. Select the Basic Bread cycle.

Nutritions *(Per serving):*

Calories: 172 kcal
Total Fat: 3.9 g

Cholesterol: 9 mg
Sodium: 155 mg

Carbohydrates: 28.9 g

Protein: 5 g

26. ITALIAN BREAD II

PREPARATION: 10 MIN   **COOKING:** 30 MIN   **SERVES:** 12

INGREDIENTS

- 3 cups unbleached all-purpose flour
- 1 tablespoon brown sugar
- 1 1/2 teaspoons salt
- 1 1/8 cups warm water (110 degrees F/45 degrees C)
- 1 1/2 tablespoons olive oil
- 1 1/2 teaspoons (active dry yeast)
- 1 egg
- 1 tablespoon water
- 1 tablespoon sesame seeds
- 1 tablespoon cornmeal

DIRECTIONS

1. Add all the ingredients except the egg, 1 tablespoon of water, sesame seeds, and cornflour into your bread maker in the order suggested by the manufacturer. Select the dough cycle.
2. Divide the batter into two parts and shape it into bread. Sprinkle cornmeal on a greased baking sheet. Place loaves on pan seam side down. Brush top of loaves with water. Let rise till double, about 50 minutes.
3. Preheat oven to 375 degrees F.
4. Brush the bread with egg wash. Sprinkle with sesame seeds. Make 4 cuts about 1/4 inch deep across the top of the log. Place a pot of hot water on the bottom of the furnace. Bake bread for 25 to 30 minutes or until golden. To make a nice crusty bread, bake bread in the afternoon and pop it into the oven again for 5 minutes before the meal.

Nutritions *(Per serving):*

Calories: 147 kcal	Cholesterol: 16 mg	Carbohydrates: 25.9 g	Protein: 4.1 g
Total Fat: 2.8 g	Sodium: 298 mg		

27. ITALIAN BREAD III

PREPARATION: 5 MIN	**COOKING:** 3 H	**SERVES:** 12

INGREDIENTS

- 1 (.25 ounce) package active dry yeast
- 3 cups bread flour
- 2 tablespoons white sugar
- 2 tablespoons margarine, softened
- 1 cup warm water
- 2 egg whites, stiffly beaten

DIRECTIONS

1. Add ingredients according to the manufacturer's directions.
2. Be sure to use the "crisp" bread setting and add the egg whites after the rest of the ingredients are moist.

Nutritions *(Per serving):*

Calories: 43 kcal	*Cholesterol: 28 mg*
Total Fat: 3 g	*Sodium: 40 mg*

Carbohydrates: 2.9 g

Protein: 1.1 g

CHAPTER 6
Grain, Seed, and Nut Bread

28. AWESOME GOLDEN CORN BREAD

PREPARATION: 10 MIN **COOKING:** 1-3 H **SERVES:** 12-16

INGREDIENTS

- 1 cup buttermilk at 80 degrees F
- 2 whole eggs, at room temperature
- ¼ cup melted butter cooled
- 1 1/3 cups all-purpose flour
- 1 cup cornmeal
- ¼ cup sugar
- 1 tablespoon baking powder
- 1 teaspoon salt

DIRECTIONS

1. Add buttermilk, butter, and eggs to your bread machine, carefully following the manufacturer's instructions.
2. Program the machine for Quick/Rapid Bread mode and press START.
3. While the wet ingredients are being mixed in the machine, take a small bowl and combine it with flour, cornmeal, sugar, baking powder, and salt.
4. After the first fast mix is done and the machine gives the signal, add dry ingredients.
5. Wait until the whole cycle completes.
6. Once the loaf is done, take the bucket out and let it cool for 5 minutes.
7. Gently shake the basket to remove the loaf and transfer to a cooling rack.
8. Slice and serve!

Nutritions *(Per serving):*

Carbohydrates: 24 g

Fiber: 2 g
Protein: 4 g

Fat: 5 g
Calories: 158 kcal

29. HEARTY OATMEAL LOAF

PREPARATION: 10 MIN   **COOKING:** 2-3 H   **SERVES:** 8

INGREDIENTS

- ¾ cup water at 80 degrees F
- 2 tablespoons melted butter, cooled
- 2 tablespoons sugar
- 1 teaspoon salt
- ¾ cup quick oats
- 1½ cups white bread flour
- 1 teaspoon instant yeast

DIRECTIONS

1. Combine all of the ingredients to your bread maker, carefully following the instructions of the manufacturer.
2. Set the program of your bread machine to Basic/White Bread and set crust type to Medium.
3. Press START.
4. Wait until the cycle completes.
5. Once the loaf is ready, take the bucket out. Chill the bread for 5 minutes.
6. Lightly shake the bucket to remove the bread.
7. Transfer on a cooling grid, slice, and serve.

Nutritions *(Per serving):*

Carbohydrates: 26 g

Fiber: 1 g
Protein: 4 g

Fat: 4 g
Calories: 149 kcal

30. CRACKED WHEAT BREAD

PREPARATION: 40MIN	**COOKING:** 2-3 H	**SERVES:** 8

INGREDIENTS

- 3 tablespoons cracked wheat
- ¾ cup + 2 tablespoons boiling water
- 2 2/3 tablespoons melted butter, cooled
- 1 teaspoon salt
- 2 tablespoons honey
- 2/3 cup whole wheat flour
- 1 1/3 cups white bread flour
- 1 1/3 teaspoons instant yeast

DIRECTIONS

1. Take the bucket of your bread machine and add cracked wheat and water; let it sit for 30 minutes until liquid is 80 degrees F.
2. Add the rest of the ingredients to your bread machine, carefully following the instructions of the manufacturer.
3. Set the program of your bread machine to Basic/White Bread and set crust type to Medium.
4. Press START.
5. Wait until the cycle completes.
6. Once the loaf is ready, take the bucket out. Chill the bread for 5 minutes.
7. Carefully shake the bucket off the bread.
8. Transfer on a cooling grid, slice, and serve.

Nutritions *(Per serving):*

Carbohydrates: 31 g	Protein: 4 g	Calories: 176 kcal
Fiber: 1 g	Fat: 4 g	

31. ORANGE ALMOND BREAD

PREPARATION: 10 MIN　　**COOKING:** 3 H 30　　**SERVES:** 16

INGREDIENTS

- 4 cups all-purpose flour
- ¾ cup sweet almonds, chopped
- 3 tablespoons brown sugar
- peels of 2 oranges, grated
- 1 cup orange juice
- 2 tablespoons sweet almond oil
- 1 teaspoon salt
- powdered sugar for sprinkling
- 2½ bread machine yeast

DIRECTIONS

1. Combine all of the ingredients to your bread machine (except the powdered sugar and ¼ cup almonds), carefully following the manufacturer's instructions.
2. Set the program of your bread machine to Basic/White Bread and set crust type to Medium.
3. Press START.
4. Wait until the cycle completes.
5. Once the loaf is ready, take the bucket out and let the loaf cool for 5 minutes.
6. Carefully shake the bucket to remove the loaf.
7. Moisten the surface with water and sprinkle with remaining almonds and powdered sugar.
8. Transfer on a cooling grid, slice, and serve.

Nutritions *(Per serving):*

Carbohydrates: 61.1 g
Fiber: 1 g

Protein: 8.5 g
Fat: 7 g

Calories: 347 kcal

32. CORN, POPPY SEEDS, AND SOUR CREAM BREAD

PREPARATION: 10 MIN   **COOKING:** 3H 30   **SERVES:** 16

INGREDIENTS

- 3½ cups wheat flour
- 1¾ cups corn flour
- 5 ounces sour cream
- 2 tablespoons corn oil
- 2 teaspoons active dried yeast
- 2 teaspoons salt
- 16 ¼ ounces water
- poppy seeds for sprinkling

DIRECTIONS

1. Add 16¼ ounces of water and corn oil to the bread maker bucket.
2. Add flour, sour cream, sugar, and salt from different angles.
3. Make a groove in the flour and add yeast.
4. Set the program of your bread machine to Basic/White Bread and set crust type to Medium.
5. Press START.
6. Wait until the cycle completes.
7. Once the bread is ready, remove the bucket and let cool for 5 minutes.
8. Carefully shake the bucket to remove the loaf.
9. Moisten the surface with water and sprinkle with poppy seeds.
10. Transfer on a cooling grid, slice, and serve.

Nutritions *(Per serving):*

Carbohydrates: 64 g   Protein: 9 g   Calories: 374 kcal
Fiber: 1 g   Fat: 10 g

33. SIMPLE DARK RYE LOAF

PREPARATION: 5 MIN   **COOKING:** 2-3 H   **SERVES:** 8

INGREDIENTS

- 2/3 cup water at 80 degrees F
- 1 tablespoon melted butter, cooled
- ¼ cup molasses
- ¼ teaspoon salt
- 1 tablespoon unsweetened cocoa powder
- ½ cup rye flour
- pinch of ground nutmeg
- 1¼ cups white bread flour
- 1 1/8 teaspoons instant yeast

DIRECTIONS

1. Combine all of the ingredients to your bread machine, carefully following the instructions of the manufacturer.
2. Set the program of your bread machine to Basic/White Bread and set crust type to Medium.
3. Press START.
4. Wait until the cycle completes.
5. Once the bread is ready, remove the bucket and let cool for 5 minutes.
6. Carefully shake the bucket to remove the loaf.
7. Transfer on a cooling grid, slice, and serve.

Nutritions *(Per serving):*

Carbohydrates: 29 g
Fiber: 1 g

Protein: 4 g
Fat: 2 g

Calories: 144 kcal

34. PISTACHIO HORSERADISH APPLE BREAD

PREPARATION: 20MIN   **COOKING:** 2-3 H   **SERVES:** 16

INGREDIENTS

- 3 cups wheat flour
- 2 whole eggs, beaten
- 3 tablespoons horseradish, grated
- ½ cup apple puree
- 1 tablespoon sugar
- 4 tablespoons olive oil
- ½ cup pistachios, peeled and chopped
- 1 teaspoon instant yeast
- 1 cup + 1 tablespoon water
- 1 teaspoon salt

DIRECTIONS

1. Lightly beat eggs in a bowl.
2. Add 1 cup + 1 tablespoons water to the bread maker bucket.
3. Add olive oil.
4. Add flour, applesauce, half of the pistachios, horseradish, and eggs into the bucket.
5. Mix well and make a small groove in the middle.
6. Add yeast.
7. Add salt and sugar to the bucket from different sides.
8. Set the program of your bread machine to Basic/White Bread and set crust type to Medium.
9. Press START.
10. Wait until the cycle completes.
11. Once the loaf is ready, take the bucket out and let the loaf cool for 5 minutes.
12. Carefully shake the bucket to remove the loaf.
13. Transfer to a cooling grid, slice, and serve.

Nutritions *(Per serving):*

Carbohydrates: 41 g
Fiber: 2 g

Protein: 8 g
Fat: 10 g

Calories: 291 kcal

35. MESMERIZING WALNUT BREAD

PREPARATION: 10 MIN   **COOKING:** 3-4 H   **SERVES:** 12-16

INGREDIENTS

- 4 cups wheat flour
- ½ cup water
- ½ cup milk
- 2 whole eggs, beaten
- ½ cup walnut
- 1 tablespoon vegetable oil
- 1 tablespoon sugar
- 1 teaspoon salt
- 1 teaspoon bread machine yeast

DIRECTIONS

1. Add milk, water, vegetable oil, and eggs to the bread maker bucket.
2. Pour in sifted wheat flour.
3. Add salt, sugar, and yeast on three sides of the bucket.
4. Set the program of your bread machine to French Bread and set crust type to Light.
5. Press START.
6. Let the kneading begin and close the lid.
7. Slightly fry the walnuts in a dry frying pan until crispy; then let them cool.
8. Once the bread maker gives the signal, add the nuts to the bread maker.
9. Mix with a spatula.
10. Let the remaining cycle complete.
11. Once the loaf is ready, take the bucket out and let the loaf cool for 5 minutes.
12. Carefully shake the bucket to remove the loaf.
13. Transfer to a cooling rack, slice, and serve.

Nutritions *(Per serving):*

Carbohydrates: 40 g
Fiber: 1 g

Protein: 9 g
Fat: 7 g

Calories: 257 kcal

36. BRAN PACKED HEALTHY BREAD

PREPARATION: 10 MIN   **COOKING:** 2-3 H   **SERVES:** 8

INGREDIENTS

- ¾ cup milk at 80 degrees F
- 1½ tablespoons melted butter, cooled
- 2 tablespoons sugar
- 1 teaspoon salt
- ¼ cup wheat bran
- 1¾ cups white bread flour
- 1 teaspoon instant yeast

DIRECTIONS

1. Combine all of the ingredients to your bread machine, carefully following the instructions of the manufacturer.
2. Set the program of your bread machine to Basic/White Bread and set crust type to Light.
3. Press START.
4. Wait until the cycle completes.
5. Once the loaf is ready, take the bucket out and let the loaf cool for 5 minutes.
6. Carefully shake the bucket to remove the loaf.
7. Transfer to a cooling rack, slice, and serve.

Nutritions *(Per serving):*

Carbohydrates: 26 g
Fiber: 1 g

Protein: 4 g
Fat: 4 g

Calories: 149 kcal

37. ORANGE WALNUT CANDIED LOAF

PREPARATION: 10 MIN | **COOKING:** 2-4 H | **SERVES:** 12

INGREDIENTS

- ½ cup warm whey
- 1 tablespoon bread machine yeast
- 4 tablespoons sugar
- 2 orange juice
- 4 cups flour
- 1 teaspoon salt
- 1½ tablespoons salt
- 3 teaspoons orange zest
- 1/3 teaspoon vanilla
- 3 tablespoons (walnut + almonds)
- ½ cup candied fruit

DIRECTIONS

1. Combine all of the ingredients to your bread machine, carefully following the instructions of the manufacturer.
2. Set the program of your bread machine to Basic/White Bread and set crust type to Medium.
3. Press START.
4. Wait until the cycle completes.
5. Once the loaf is ready, take the bucket out and let the loaf cool for 5 minutes.
6. Carefully shake the bucket to remove the loaf.
7. Transfer to a cooling rack, slice, and serve.

Nutritions *(Per serving):*

Carbohydrates: 82 g
Fiber: 1 g

Protein: 12 g
Fat: 7 g

Calories: 437 kcal

38. CARAMEL APPLE PECAN LOAF

PREPARATION: 10 MIN	**COOKING:** 3 H 50	**SERVES:** 8

INGREDIENTS

- 1 cup water
- 2 tablespoons butter
- 3 cups bread flour
- ¼ cup packed brown sugar
- ¾ teaspoon ground cinnamon
- 1 teaspoon salt
- 2 teaspoons quick yeast
- ½ cup apple, chopped
- 1/3 cup coarsely chopped pecans, toasted

DIRECTIONS

1. Combine all of the ingredients to your bread machine (except apples and pecans), carefully following the manufacturer's instructions.
2. Set the program of your bread machine to Basic/White Bread and set crust type to Medium.
3. Press START.
4. Once the bread maker beeps, add pecans and apples.
5. Wait until the cycle completes.
6. Once the loaf is ready, take the bucket out and let the loaf cool for 5 minutes.
7. Carefully shake the bucket to remove the loaf.
8. Transfer to a cooling rack, slice, and serve.

Nutritions *(Per serving):*

57

Carbohydrates: 32 g	Protein: 4 g	Calories: 185 kcal
Fiber: 2 g	Fat: 5 g	

39. SESAME SEEDS AND ONION BREAD

PREPARATION: 10 MIN   **COOKING:** 2-3 H   **SERVES:** 20

INGREDIENTS

- ¾ cup water
- 32/3 cups flour
- ¾ cup cottage cheese
- 2 tablespoons soft butter
- 2 tablespoons sugar
- 1½ teaspoons salt
- 1½ tablespoons sesame seeds
- 2 tablespoons dried onion
- 1¼ teaspoons dry yeast

DIRECTIONS

1. Combine all of the ingredients to your bread machine, carefully following the instructions of the manufacturer.
2. Set the program of your bread machine to Basic/White Bread and set crust type to Medium.
3. Press START.
4. Wait until the cycle completes.
5. Once the loaf is ready, take the bucket out and let the loaf cool for 5 minutes.
6. Carefully shake the bucket to remove the loaf.
7. Transfer to a cooling rack, slice, and serve.

Nutritions *(Per serving):*

Carbohydrates: 48 g
Fiber: 2 g

Protein: 10 g
Fat: 5 g

Calories: 277 kcal

40. AWESOME MULTIGRAIN BREAD

PREPARATION: 10 MIN   **COOKING:** 2-3 H   **SERVES:** 8

INGREDIENTS

- ¾ cup water at 80 degrees F
- 1 tablespoon melted butter
- ½ tablespoon honey
- ½ teaspoon salt
- ¾ cup multigrain flour
- 11/3 cups white bread flour
- 1 teaspoon active dry yeast

DIRECTIONS

1. Combine all of the ingredients to your bread machine, carefully following the instructions of the manufacturer.
2. Set the program of your bread machine to Basic/White Bread and set crust type to Medium.
3. Press START.
4. Wait until the cycle completes.
5. Once the loaf is ready, take the bucket out and let the loaf cool for 5 minutes.
6. Carefully shake the bucket to remove the loaf.
7. Transfer to a cooling rack, slice, and serve.

Nutritions *(Per serving):*

Carbohydrates: 27 g   Protein: 4 g   Calories: 145 kcal
Fiber: 2 g   Fat: 2 g

41. DELICIOUS RICE BREAD

PREPARATION: 15 MIN   **COOKING:** 3H 30 MIN   **SERVES:** 16

INGREDIENTS

- 4½ cups wheat flour
- 1 cup rice, cooked
- 1 whole egg, beaten
- 2 tablespoons milk powder
- 2 teaspoons active dry yeast
- 2 tablespoons butter
- 1 tablespoon sugar
- 2 teaspoon salt
- 1 ¼ cups water

DIRECTIONS

1. Add 1¼ cups water to the bread maker bucket.
2. Add beaten egg.
3. Add flour, rice, and milk powder.
4. Add butter, sugar, and salt in different corners of the bucket.
5. Make a groove in the middle of the flour and add yeast.
6. Set the program of your bread machine to Basic/White Bread and set crust type to Medium.
7. Press START.
8. Wait until the cycle completes.
9. Once the loaf is ready, take the bucket out and let the loaf cool for 5 minutes.
10. Carefully shake the bucket to remove the loaf.
11. Transfer to a cooling rack, slice, and serve.

Nutritions *(Per serving):*

Carbohydrates: 61 g   Protein: 9 g   Calories: 328 kcal
Fiber: 1 g   Fat: 5 g

42. SUNFLOWER SEEDS AND OATMEAL BREAD

PREPARATION: 15 MIN   **COOKING:** 3-4 H   **SERVES:** 8

INGREDIENTS

- 1 cup water
- ¼ cup honey
- 2 tablespoons butter
- 3 cups bread flour
- ½ cup quick-cooking oats
- 2 tablespoons dry milk
- 1¼ teaspoons salt
- 2¼ teaspoons bread machine yeast
- ½ cup sunflower seeds

DIRECTIONS

1. Combine all of the ingredients to your bread machine, carefully following the manufacturer's instructions (except seeds.)
2. Set the program of your bread machine to Basic/White Bread and set crust type to Light.
3. Press START.
4. Once the machine beeps, add seeds.
5. Wait until the cycle completes.
6. Once the loaf is ready, take the bucket out and let the loaf cool for 5 minutes.
7. Carefully shake the bucket to remove the loaf.
8. Transfer to a cooling rack, slice, and serve.

Nutritions *(Per serving):*

Carbohydrates: 36 g
Fiber: 1 g

Protein: 6 g
Fat: 5 g

Calories: 200 kcal

43. SUNFLOWER WALNUT BREAD

PREPARATION: 10 MIN   **COOKING:** 3H 30 MIN   **SERVES:** 28

INGREDIENTS

- 1 1/3 cups hot water
- 2 tablespoons powdered milk
- 2 tablespoons olive oil
- 3 tablespoons honey
- 1 ½ tsp sea salt
- 3 ¾ cups bread flour
- 1/3 cup sunflower seed kernels
- 1/3 cup walnuts, finely diced
- 1 ½ tsp bread machine yeast
- 2 tsp vital wheat gluten

DIRECTIONS

1. Add ingredients to the pan.
2. Choose basic bread setting and light/medium crust color.
3. After removing from pan and cooling, brush sides with butter to prevent the crust from hardening.
4. Cool again before serving.

Nutritions *(Per serving):*

Calories: 45 kcal
Fat: 2.6 g

Sodium: 149 mg
Carbohydrates: 4 g

Fiber: 4 g
Protein: 1 g

44. BRAZIL NUT AND NUTMEG BREAD

PREPARATION: 10 MIN | **COOKING:** 3 H | **SERVES:** 12

INGREDIENTS

- 1 1/4 cups water
- 2 tablespoon oil
- 3 cups whole meal bread flour
- 1 1/2 tsp salt
- 2 tsp white sugar
- 1 tsp freshly grated nutmeg
- 1 1/2 tsp instant or fast-acting dried yeast
- 7/8 cup Brazil nuts, coarsely chopped

DIRECTIONS

1. Add ingredients to the pan except for Brazil nuts.
2. Choose a basic bread setting.
3. Add nuts at prompt.
4. Cool before slicing and serving.

Nutritions *(Per serving):*

Calories: 98 kcal
Fat: 6.7 g

Sodium: 356 mg
Carbohydrates: 7.4 g

Fiber: 1.3 g
Protein: 2.7 g

45. ALMOND BREAD

PREPARATION: 10 MIN | **COOKING:** 3 H | **SERVES:** 12

INGREDIENTS

- 1 ¼ cups water
- 4 tsp almond oil
- 1 tsp salt
- ¼ cup honey
- 1 cup almond flour
- 2 cups whole wheat flour
- ¼ cup vital wheat gluten
- 1 tsp xanthan gum
- 1 (.25 oz.) package dry yeast

DIRECTIONS

1. Combine the above ingredients, respectively, as ordered.
2. Choose bread setting—check the manufacture's guidelines for a 2 lbs. loaf.

Nutritions *(Per serving):*

Calories: 117 kcal
Fat: 1.9 g

Sodium: 206 mg
Carbohydrates: 22 g

Fiber: 3 g
Protein: 4.6 g

46. PECAN WALNUT BREAD

PREPARATION: 10 MIN   **COOKING:** 3 H 35 MIN   **SERVES:** 12

INGREDIENTS

- 2 tsp instant yeast
- 1 cup + 2 tablespoons water
- 3 tablespoons dark brown sugar
- 2 tablespoons butter
- 2 cups bread flour
- 1 cup whole wheat flour
- 1 ¼ tsp salt
- 1 cup diced pecans and walnuts

DIRECTIONS

1. Add in all ingredients into the bread machine in order the manufacturer recommends.
2. Choose the basic cycle and start.
3. Roughly 10 minutes into the kneading cycle, check the dough's consistency, adding dough or water as recommended to allow the formation of a smooth and soft dough ball.
4. Let the machine complete the cycle.
5. Cool bread before serving.

Nutritions *(Per serving):*

Calories: 137 kcal
Fat: 8.6 g

Sodium: 316 mg
Carbohydrates: 14.18 g

Fiber: 1.3 g
Protein: 2.6 g

47. SEVEN GRAIN BREAD

PREPARATION: 10 MIN   **COOKING:** 3 H   **SERVES:** 16

INGREDIENTS

- 1 1/3 cups warm water
- 1 tablespoon active dry yeast
- 3 tablespoons dry milk powder
- 2 tablespoons vegetable oil
- 2 tablespoons honey
- 2 tsp salt
- 1 egg
- 1 cup whole wheat flour
- 2 ½ cups bread flour
- 3/4 cup 7-grain cereal

DIRECTIONS

1. Add ingredients to the pan.
2. Choose whole-wheat bread cycle.

Nutritions *(Per serving):*

Calories: 47 kcal
Fat: 5.2 g

Sodium: 629 mg
Carbohydrates: 50 g

Fiber: 3.5 g
Protein: 9.8 g

48. QUINOA OATMEAL BREAD

PREPARATION: 10 MIN **COOKING:** 3 H 50 MIN **SERVES:** 12

INGREDIENTS

- 1/3 cup uncooked quinoa (or 1/2 cup quinoa flakes)
- 2/3 cup water for quinoa grains—not needed if using flakes
- 1 cup buttermilk
- 1 tsp salt
- 1 tablespoon sugar
- 1 tablespoon honey
- 4 tablespoons butter
- 1/2 cup quick oats
- 1/2 cup whole wheat flour
- 1 ½ cups bread flour
- 1 ½ tsp yeast

DIRECTIONS

1. Cook quinoa grains; bring to a boil for 5 minutes covered. Turn off the heat and let sit for 10 minutes. * skip if using flakes.
2. Add ingredients to the pan.
3. Choose whole-wheat bread cycle.

Nutritions *(Per serving):*

Calories: 48 kcal
Fat: 4.7 g

Sodium: 307 mg
Carbohydrates: 12.54 g

Fiber: 1.3 g
Protein: 2.9 g

CHAPTER 7
Sourdough Bread

49. EASY SOURDOUGH BREAD

PREPARATION: 3 MIN | **COOKING:** 3 H | **SERVES:** 16

INGREDIENTS

- 2 2/3 cups bread flour
- 1 cup sourdough starter
- ¾ cup warm water
- 1½ teaspoons active dry yeast
- 1½ teaspoons salt

DIRECTIONS

1. Add all the ingredients to your bread machine pan according to the order suggested by the manufacturer.
2. Select white bread setting and press start.

Nutritions *(Per serving):*

| Calories: 84 kcal | Sodium: 234 mg | 17.35 g | Fiber: 0.7 g |
| Fat: 0.28 g | Carbohydrates: | Protein: 2.57 g | Sugar: 0.13 g |

50. BASIC SOURDOUGH BREAD

PREPARATION: 15 MIN   **COOKING:** 3 H   **SERVES:** 12

INGREDIENTS

- 1 1/3 cups sourdough starter
- 1 2/3 cups all-purpose flour
- 2 tablespoons lukewarm water
- 1 tablespoon vegetable oil
- 1 teaspoon instant or active dry yeast
- 1 teaspoon sugar
- 1 teaspoon salt

DIRECTIONS

1. Add all the ingredients to your bread machine pan according to the order suggested by the manufacturer.
2. Select the basic cycle and press start.

Nutritions *(Per serving):*

Calories: 98 kcal	*Sodium: 245 mg*	*17.95 g*	*Fiber: 0.7 g*
Fat: 1.53 g	*Carbohydrates:*	*Protein: 2.83 g*	*Sugar: 0.64 g*

51. YOUR EVERYDAY SOURDOUGH BREAD

PREPARATION: 10 MIN	**COOKING:** 3 H	**SERVES:** 12

INGREDIENTS

- 3 cups bread flour
- 1 cup sourdough starter
- ½ cup water
- 2 tablespoons sugar
- 1½ teaspoons salt
- 1 teaspoon quick active dry yeast

VEGAN

DIRECTIONS

1. Add all the ingredients to your bread machine pan according to the order suggested by the manufacturer.
2. Select the basic or white cycle and press start.

Nutritions *(Per serving):*

Calories: 120 kcal
Fat: 0.33 g
Sodium: 292 mg

Carbohydrates: 25.31 g
Protein: 3.36 g
Fiber: 0.9 g

Sugar: 1.39 g

52. SOURDOUGH WHOLE WHEAT BREAD

PREPARATION: 5 MIN	**COOKING:** 3 H	**SERVES:** 18

INGREDIENTS

- 4 cups whole wheat flour
- 1¼ cups whole wheat sourdough starter
- 1 cup plus 3 tablespoons water
- 2 tablespoons plus 2 teaspoons vegetable oil
- 1 tablespoon plus 1 teaspoon sugar
- 1 tablespoon active dry yeast
- 2 teaspoons salt

DIRECTIONS

1. Add all the ingredients to your bread machine pan according to the order suggested by the manufacturer.
2. Select basic or whole wheat cycle and press start.

Nutritions *(Per serving):*

Calories: 141 kcal
Fat: 2.24 g
Sodium: 266 mg

Carbohydrates: 25.1 g
Protein: 9.18 g
Fiber: 6.6 g

Sugar: 0.25 g

53. SOURDOUGH YEAST BREAD

PREPARATION: 10 MIN   **COOKING:** 3 H   **SERVES:** 14

INGREDIENTS

- 2 cups whole wheat flour
- 1¾ cups sourdough starter
- 1 cup all-purpose flour
- ¼ cup warm water
- 2 tablespoons unsalted butter
- 2 tablespoons honey or molasses
- 2¼ teaspoons active dry yeast
- 2 teaspoons salt

DIRECTIONS

1. Add all the ingredients to your bread machine pan according to the order suggested by the manufacturer.
2. Select whole wheat setting and press start.

Nutritions *(Per serving):*

Calories: 190 kcal	Sodium: 346 mg	31.78 g	Fiber: 8.7 g
Fat: 3.49 g	Carbohydrates:	Protein: 13.23 g	Sugar: 2.56 g

54. QUICK SOURDOUGH BREAD

PREPARATION: 5 MIN   **COOKING:** 4 H 30 MIN   **SERVES:** 16

INGREDIENTS

- 3¼ cups bread flour
- ½ cup plain Greek yogurt
- 2/3 cup water
- 1 tablespoon sugar or honey
- 1 tablespoon lemon juice
- 1 tablespoon unsalted butter softened
- 3 teaspoons dry yeast
- 1½ teaspoons salt

DIRECTIONS

1. Add all the ingredients to your bread machine pan according to the order suggested by the manufacturer.
2. Select whole wheat setting and press start.

Nutritions *(Per serving):*

Calories: 110 kcal	Sodium: 253 mg	27.02 g	Fiber: 0.7 g
Fat: 0.96 g	Carbohydrates:	Protein: 3.74 g	Sugar: 0.65 g

55. MULTI-GRAIN SOURDOUGH BREAD

PREPARATION: 5 MIN   **COOKING:** 3H   **SERVES:** 13

INGREDIENTS

- 3 cups unbleached white all-purpose flour
- 2/3 cup 7-grain hot cereal
- 2/3 cup water
- ¾ cup sourdough starter
- 2½ tablespoons packed brown sugar
- 1½ tablespoons unsalted butter or margarine
- 1 tablespoon water or flour
- 1 tablespoon vital wheat gluten
- 1½ teaspoons active dry yeast
- ¾ teaspoon sea salt

DIRECTIONS

1. Add all the ingredients to your bread machine pan according to the order suggested by the manufacturer.
2. Select basic bread cycle and press start.

Nutritions *(Per serving):*

Calories: 283 kcal
Fat: 1.65 g
Sodium: 148 mg

Carbohydrates: 63.87 g
Protein: 4.09 g
Fiber: 0.9 g

Sugar: 41.12 g

56. SOURDOUGH RYE BREAD

PREPARATION: 15 MIN	**COOKING:** 3 H	**SERVES:** 8

INGREDIENTS

- 1½ cups rye flour
- 1 cup bread flour
- 1 cup non-dairy milk
- 1 cup sourdough starter
- ½ cup half-baked potato, grated
- ¾ cup wheat flour
- 5 tablespoons wheat gluten
- 1 tablespoon honey
- 1 tablespoon salt
- 2 teaspoons caraway seeds

DIRECTIONS

1. Add all the ingredients to your bread machine pan according to the order suggested by the manufacturer.
2. Select dough cycle and press start.

Nutritions *(Per serving):*

Calories: 190 kcal

Fat: 1.45 g

Sodium: 938 mg

Carbohydrates: 38.99 g

Protein: 5.57 g

Fiber: 3.1 g

Sugar: 4.71 g

57. SOURDOUGH LOAF

PREPARATION: 15 MIN   **COOKING:** 3 H   **SERVES:** 18

INGREDIENTS

- 3½ cups all-purpose flour, divided
- 1 cup sourdough starter
- ¾ cup warm milk
- 2 tablespoons sugar
- 1½ tablespoons soft butter
- 2¼ teaspoons active dry yeast
- 2 teaspoons salt

DIRECTIONS

1. In a bread machine pan, add a cup of flour, yeast, sugar, and salt. Select basic bread cycle to combine the Ingredients.
2. Add the butter and milk to the flour mix slowly while the machine is still stirring. Repeat the process with the sourdough starter.
3. Add the remaining flour and close the machine so it can finish baking.

Nutritions *(Per serving):*

Calories: 112 kcal
Fat: 1.48 g
Sodium: 283 mg

Carbohydrates: 21.08 g
Protein: 3.26 g
Fiber: 0.8 g

Sugar: 1.53 g

58. PUMPERNICKEL BREAD

PREPARATION: 2 H 10	**COOKING:** 50 MIN	**SERVES:** 14

INGREDIENTS

- 1 1/8 cups warm water
- 1 ½ tablespoon vegetable oil
- 1/3 cup molasses
- 3 tablespoons cocoa
- 1 tablespoon caraway seed (optional)
- 1 ½ teaspoon salt
- 1 ½ cups bread flour
- 1 cup rye flour
- 1 cup whole wheat flour
- 1 ½ tablespoon vital wheat gluten (optional)
- 2 ½ teaspoon bread machine yeast

DIRECTIONS

1. Combine all ingredients to the bread machine pan.
2. Choose a basic bread cycle.
3. Take the bread out to cool and enjoy!

Nutritions *(Per serving):*

Calories: 97 kcal
Fat: 1 g

Carbohydrates: 19 g
Protein: 3 g

59. SAUERKRAUT RYE

PREPARATION: 2 H 20	**COOKING:** 50 MIN	**SERVES:** 12

INGREDIENTS

- 1 cup sauerkraut, rinsed and drained
- ¾ cup warm water
- 1½ tablespoons molasses
- 1½ tablespoons butter
- 1½ tablespoons brown sugar
- 1 teaspoon caraway seeds
- 1½ teaspoons salt
- 1 cup rye flour
- 2 cups bread flour
- 1½ teaspoons active dry yeast

DIRECTIONS

1. Combine all of the ingredients to your bread machine.
2. Set the program of your bread machine to Basic/White Bread and set crust type to Medium.
3. Press START.
4. Wait until the cycle completes.
5. Once the loaf is ready, take the bucket out and let the loaf cool for 5 minutes.
6. Carefully shake the bucket to remove the loaf.
7. Transfer to a cooling rack, slice, and serve.

Nutritions *(Per serving):*

Calories: 74 kcal
Fat: 2 g

Carbohydrates: 12 g
Protein: 2 g

Fiber: 1 g

60. CRUSTY SOURDOUGH BREAD

PREPARATION: 15 MIN   **COOKING:** 3 H   **SERVES:** 12

INGREDIENTS

- 1/2 cup water
- 3 cups bread flour
- 2 tablespoons sugar
- 1 ½ teaspoon salt
- 1 teaspoon a bread machine yeast or quick active dry yeast

VEGAN

DIRECTIONS

1. Measure 1 cup starter and remaining bread ingredients, add to bread machine pan.
2. Choose basic/white bread cycle with medium or light crust color.

Nutritions *(Per serving):*

Calories: 165 kcal
Carbohydrates: 37 g

Total Fat: 0 g
Protein: 5 g

Sodium: 300 mg
Fiber: 1 g

61. HONEY SOURDOUGH BREAD

PREPARATION: 15 MIN   **COOKING:** 3 H   **SERVES:** 10

INGREDIENTS

- 2/3 cup sourdough starter
- 1/2 cup water
- 1 tablespoon vegetable oil
- 2 tablespoons honey
- 1/2 teaspoon salt
- 1/2 cup high protein wheat flour
- 2 cups bread flour
- 1 teaspoon active dry yeast

DIRECTIONS

1. Measure 1 cup starter and remaining bread ingredients, add to bread machine pan.
2. Choose basic/white bread cycle with medium or light crust color.

Nutritions *(Per serving):*

Calories: 175 kcal   *Fat: 0.3 g*   *Sodium: 121 mg*
Carbohydrates: 33 g   *Protein: 5.6 g*   *Fiber: 1.9 g*

62. MULTIGRAIN SOURDOUGH BREAD

PREPARATION: 15 MIN	**COOKING:** 3 H	**SERVES:** 14

INGREDIENTS

- 2 cups sourdough starter
- 2 tablespoons butter or 2 tablespoons olive oil
- 1/2 cup milk
- 1 teaspoon salt
- 1/4 cup honey
- 1/2 cup sunflower seeds
- 1/2 cup millet or 1/2cup amaranth or 1/2cup quinoa
- 3 1/2 cups multi-grain flour

DIRECTIONS

1. Add ingredients to bread machine pan.
2. Choose the dough cycle.
3. Conventional Oven: When the cycle is complete, remove dough and place on a lightly floured surface, and shape into a loaf.
4. Place in the greased loaf pan, cover, and rise until bread is a couple of inches above the edge.
5. Bake at 375 degrees for 40 to 50 minutes.

Nutritions *(Per serving):*

Calories: 110 kcal
Carbohydrates: 13.5 g

Fat: 1.8 g
Protein: 2.7 g

Sodium: 213 mg
Fiber: 1.4 g

63. OLIVE AND GARLIC SOURDOUGH BREAD

PREPARATION: 15 MIN | **COOKING:** 3 H | **SERVES:** 12

INGREDIENTS

- 2 cups sourdough starter
- 3 cups flour
- 2 tablespoons olive oil
- 2 tablespoons sugar
- 2 teaspoon salt
- 1/2 cup chopped black olives
- 6 cloves chopped garlic

DIRECTIONS

1. Add starter and bread ingredients to the bread machine pan.
2. Choose the dough cycle.
3. Conventional Oven: Preheat oven to 350 degrees.
4. When the cycle is complete, if the dough is sticky, add more flour.
5. Shape dough onto the baking sheet or put into loaf pan
6. Bake for 35- 45 minutes until golden.
7. Cool before slicing.

VEGAN

Nutritions *(Per serving):*

Calories: 150 kcal
Carbohydrates: 26.5 g

Fat: 0.5 g
Protein: 3.4 g

Sodium: 267 mg
Fiber: 1.1 g

64. CZECH SOURDOUGH BREAD

PREPARATION: 15 MIN   **COOKING:** 3 H   **SERVES:** 15

INGREDIENTS

- 1 cup non-dairy milk
- 1 tablespoon salt
- 1 tablespoon honey
- 1 cup sourdough starter
- 1 1/2cups rye flour
- 1 cup bread flour
- 3/4 cup wheat flour
- 1/2 cup grated half-baked potato
- 5 tablespoons wheat gluten
- 2 teaspoons caraway seeds

DIRECTIONS

1. Add ingredients to bread machine pan.
2. Choose the dough cycle.
3. The dough should stand, up to 24 hours, in the bread maker until it doubles in size.
4. After rising, bake in the bread machine for one hour.

Nutritions *(Per serving):*

Calories: 198 kcal
Carbohydrates: 39.9 g

Fat: 0.8 g
Protein: 6.5 g

Sodium: 888 mg
Fiber: 4.3 g

65. FRENCH SOURDOUGH BREAD

PREPARATION: 15 MIN   **COOKING:** 3 H   **SERVES:** 16

INGREDIENTS

- 2 cups sourdough starter
- 1 teaspoon salt
- 1/2cup water
- 4 cups white bread flour
- 2 tablespoons white cornmeal

DIRECTIONS

1. Add ingredients to bread machine pan, saving cornmeal for later.
2. Choose the dough cycle.
3. Conventional Oven: Preheat oven to 375 degrees.
4. At the end of the dough cycle, turn the dough out onto a floured surface.
5. Add flour if the dough is sticky.
6. Divide dough into two portions and flatten into an oval shape 1 ½ inch thick.
7. Fold ovals in half lengthwise and pinch seams to elongate.
8. Sprinkle cornmeal onto the baking sheet and place the loaves seam side down.
9. Cover and let rise in until about doubled.
10. Place a shallow pan of hot water on the lower shelf of the oven;
11. Use a knife to make shallow, diagonal slashes in tops of loaves
12. Put the bread into the oven and spray it with a fine water mist. Spray the oven walls as well.
13. Repeat spraying 3 times at one-minute intervals.
14. Remove pan of water after 15 minutes of baking
15. Fully bake for 30 to 40 minutes or until golden brown.

Nutritions *(Per serving):*

Calories: 937 kcal
Carbohydrates: 196 g

Fat: 0.4 g
Protein: 26.5 g

Sodium: 1172 mg
Fiber: 7.3 g

CHAPTER 8
Cheese Bread

66. CHEESE HERB BREAD

PREPARATION: 15 MIN	**COOKING:** 2-4 H	**SERVES:** 10

INGREDIENTS

- 2 cups water warm water (110 degrees F/45 degrees C)
- 6 cups bread flour
- 1/4 cup sugar white sugar
- 2 teaspoons salt
- 1/4 cup dry milk powder dry milk powder
- 1/4 cup butter softened
- 6 tablespoons Parmesan cheese grated Parmesan cheese
- 2 teaspoons marjoram dried marjoram
- 2 teaspoons thyme dried thyme
- 2 teaspoons basil dried basil
- 2 teaspoons oregano dried oregano
- 2 tablespoons yeast active dry yeast

DIRECTIONS

1. Combine all ingredients in the bread machine pan in the order suggested by the product manufacturer.
2. Choose the Basic or White Bread cycle and press Start.

Nutritions *(Per serving):*

Calories: 208 kcal
Protein: 5.31 g

Fat: 10.62 g
Carbohydrates: 22.86 g

67. COTTAGE CHEESE BREAD I

PREPARATION: 10 MIN   **COOKING:** 2-4 H   **SERVES:** 10

INGREDIENTS

- 1 cup water
- 2 cups cottage cheese
- 1/4 cup margarine
- 2 eggs
- 1/2 teaspoon baking soda
- 2 teaspoons salt
- 2 tablespoons white sugar
- 6 cups bread flour
- 1 1/2 tablespoons active dry yeast

DIRECTIONS

1. Combine the ingredients to your bread machine in the order suggested by the product manufacturer and start.
2. You may use up to 1/2 cup more bread flour if the dough appears too sticky.

Nutritions *(Per serving):*

Calories: 204 kcal
Protein: 5.21 g

Fat: 10.42 g
Carbohydrates: 22.42 g

68. CHEDDAR CHEESE BREAD

PREPARATION: 10 MIN   **COOKING:** 2-4 H   **SERVES:** 10

INGREDIENTS

- 2 (.25 ounce) package active dry yeast
- 1/2 cup dry milk powder
- 2 tablespoons butter, softened
- 6 cups bread flour
- 2 teaspoons salt
- 1/4 cup white sugar
- 2 1/2 cups warm water
- 3 cups shredded sharp Cheddar cheese

DIRECTIONS

1. Combine the ingredients in the pan of the bread machine in the order recommended by the product manufacturer.
2. Select White Bread setting; press Start.

Nutritions *(Per serving):*

Calories: 212 kcal
Protein: 5.42 g

Fat: 10.83 g
Carbohydrates: 23.31 g

69. CREAM CHEESE YEAST BREAD

PREPARATION: 10 MIN   **COOKING:** 2-4 H   **SERVES:** 10

INGREDIENTS

- 1 cup water
- 1 cup cream cheese, softened
- 2 beaten eggs
- 8 tablespoons sugar
- 4 tablespoons melted butter
- 2 teaspoon salt
- 6 cups bread flour
- 3 teaspoons active dry yeast

DIRECTIONS

1. Combine the ingredients in the pan in the sequence suggested by your bread machine manufacturer.
2. A process on the dough cycle.
3. Remove from machine, form right into a loaf, and place in greased 9x5 loaf pan.
4. Cover and let rise until doubled.
5. Bake in a 350 degree F oven for about 35 minutes.

Nutritions *(Per serving):*

Calories: 210 kcal
Protein: 5.34 g

Fat: 10.65 g
Carbohydrates: 22.80 g

70. ONION, GARLIC, CHEESE BREAD

PREPARATION: 10 MIN	**COOKING:** 2-4 H	**SERVES:** 10

INGREDIENTS

- 2 1/4 cups warm water
- 6 cups bread flour
- 1/4 cup dry milk powder
- 1 tablespoon salt
- 1/4 cup margarine
- 1/4 cup white sugar
- 1 1/2 tablespoons active dry yeast
- 1 1/2 tablespoons garlic powder
- 6 tablespoons dried minced onions
- 2 cups shredded sharp Cheddar cheese

DIRECTIONS

1. Add water, flour, powdered milk, sugar, salt, butter or margarine, and yeast into the bread machine in the order suggested by your manufacturer. Set for the basic cycle using the light crust.
2. When indicated by your manufacturer, add the garlic powder, 2 tablespoons the onion flakes, and every shredded cheese. Following the last knead, sprinkle the rest of the tablespoon of onion flakes over the dough.
3. Enjoy hot and fresh bread.

Nutritions *(Per serving):*

Calories: 215 kcal
Protein: 5.11 g

Fat: 10.60 g
Carbohydrates: 22.76 g

71. PEPPERONI CHEESE BREAD

PREPARATION: 15 MIN   **COOKING:** 2-4 H   **SERVES:** 10

INGREDIENTS

- 2 cups water (70° to 80°)
- 2 tablespoons butter
- 1 1/2 tablespoons ground mustard
- 1 teaspoon salt
- 1/4 cup sugar
- 1 teaspoon cayenne pepper
- 1/2 teaspoon garlic powder
- 6 cups bread flour
- 1 1/2 tablespoons 2-1/4 active dry yeast
- 3 cups 1-1/2 shredded Mexican cheese blend
- 2 cups chopped pepperoni

DIRECTIONS

1. Put the first 9 ingredients into the bread pan in the sequence suggested by the manufacturer. Select basic bread setting. Choose crust color and loaf size if available. Bake according to bread machine directions (check dough after 5 minutes of mixing; add 1 to 2 tablespoons of water or flour if needed).
2. Before the final kneading (your machine may audibly signal this), add the cheese and pepperoni. Freeze option: Securely wrap and freeze cooled loaf in foil and place in a resealable plastic freezer bag. To use, thaw at room temperature.

Nutritions *(Per serving):*

Calories: 230 kcal
Protein: 5.42 g

Fat: 10.31 g
Carbohydrates: 22.45 g

72. BASIL BREAD WITH TOMATO AND MOZZARELLA CHEESE RECIPE

PREPARATION: 10MIN   **COOKING:** 2-4 H   **SERVES:** 16

INGREDIENTS

- 1 cup 80 ° F. / 27 ° C hot.
- 3 tbsp. of olive oil
- 1 cup chopped tomatoes drained
- One-fourth cups shredded mozzarella cheese (optional)
- 2.50 tbsp. of sugar
- 1.75 tsp salt
- Four cups bread flour 2 tsp shredded fresh basil or four teaspoons of dried basil 2 1/4teaspoon bread maker yeast

DIRECTIONS

1. Place the ingredients into the bread pan, as shown in the ingredients list, and select the simple or white course, 2-pound bread, and medium crust.
2. If the dough appears a little loose due to tomatoes' addition, apply some flour one tablespoon at a time during the kneading process to obtain the right consistency. You may also sprinkle basil on top of the loaf before beginning the growing process.
3. When the loaf has finished, remove it from the bread pan and let it rest for 10 minutes on a cooling rack, cut it into slices, and then serve it.
4. Great to eat alone and great with a pasta course or a big green salad.

Nutritions *(Per serving):*

Calories: 222 kcal
Protein: 5.12 g

Fat: 10.22 g
Carbohydrates: 22.36 g

73. BLUE CHEESE POTATO BREAD RECIPE

PREPARATION: 10 MIN   **COOKING:** 2-4 H   **SERVES:** 12

INGREDIENTS

- One plus 1/4 cup water (110 ° F. /43 ° C.)
- One egg (room temperature)
- One tablespoon melted butter
- 1/4 cup non-fat dried milk powder
- One tablespoon sugar
- 3/4 teaspoon salt
- Half teaspoon onion powder
- 1/2 cup crumbled blue cheese
- 3 cups bread flour
- 1/3 cup mashed potato flakes or buds
- One teaspoon active dry yeast or bread machine yeast

DIRECTIONS

1. Adding ingredients to the bread machine and select white bread 1.5-pound loaf and dark crust button.
2. Remove loaf from the bread pan. Let it cool and serve.

Nutritions *(Per serving):*

Calories: 210 kcal
Protein: 4.91 g

Fat: 12.10 g
Carbohydrates: 23.25 g

74. BACON ONION CHEESE BREAD RECIPE

PREPARATION: 10 MIN | **COOKING:** 2-4 H | **SERVES:** 8

INGREDIENTS

Dough:
- 1 cup 110 ° F milk. /43 degrees.
- 1 tsp salt
- 2 tsp onion powder
- 2 tbsp. Softened butter
- 3 1/4cups bread flour
- 2 tsp. Bread machine or active dry yeast

Filling:
- 16 ounces (one pound) of sliced bacon
- 1 1/2 cups finely diced onions
- 1/2 teaspoon black pepper
- One teaspoon paprika
- One cup shredded parmesan or asiago cheese

For glaze and pan:
- One large egg with 1 tbsp. Of water for the glaze.
- One tablespoon bacon fat to glaze pan

DIRECTIONS

1. Put the ingredients for the bread dough into the bread machine pan and choose the dough setting. Add the ingredients in the order set out in the list of ingredients.
2. Prepare the bacon/onion/cheese stuffing while the bread machine is making the dough.
3. Cook the bacon till it is crispy and drain away to a plate covered with paper towels. Reserve the bacon fat for three tablespoons. Cut the bacon into pieces, and put it in a dish.
4. Cook the onions until crispy and caramelize the bacon drippings in 2 teaspoons. Drain on the paper towels and apply the pepper, paprika, and shredded cheese to the bacon in the bowl and shake. Book it until later. Put aside 1/3 of this mixture, after glazing with egg wash, to cover the crust.
5. Roll the bread dough out to an 8 x 18-inch rectangle after the dough process is complete. Clean some of the egg wash and scatter some of the fillings over the floor. Roll the dough and put in a baking pan of 9 x 5 inches of bread, oiled with some of the bacon fat. Glaze the top of the bread and top with the remaining topping to rise for 45 minutes to an hour. Preheat the oven to 350 ° F/ 145 ° C and bake until browned for 30 minutes.
6. Let rest and slice for 10 minutes, and serve.

Nutritions *(Per serving):*

Calories: 265 kcal
Protein: 5.21 g

Fat: 13.12 g
Carbohydrates: 24.25 g

75. ASIAGO CHEESE BREAD RECIPE

PREPARATION: 10 MIN   **COOKING:** 2-4 H   **SERVES:** 16

INGREDIENTS

- One ¼ cup 110 ° F/43 ° C milk
- 1 1/2Tsp salt
- One tsp sugar
- ¼ tsp pepper
- Two tablespoons butter
- One large egg
- 4 cups bread flour or all-purpose flour
- 1 1/4cup shredded asiago cheese (topping save 1/4cup)
- 1/2tsp. of Bread-machine yeast or active dry yeast

DIRECTIONS

1. Place the ingredients to the machine pan in the order specified in the ingredients part and pick basic white-bread, 2-pound loaf, and medium crust framework. Reserve a 1/4cup of the Asiago grated cheese.
2. Top the risen dough with the remaining 1/4cup of shredded asiago cheese after the rising process and before the baking cycle starts, close the lid quickly.
3. Let the bread cool for ten minutes, slice, and serve.

Nutritions *(Per serving):*

Calories: 270 kcal
Protein: 4.55 g

Fat: 14.10 g
Carbohydrates: 25.60 g

76. CHEESE AND BEER BREAD RECIPE

PREPARATION: 15 MIN   **COOKING:** 2-4 H   **SERVES:** 12

INGREDIENTS

- Ten ounces of beer, at room temperature
- Four ounces of shredded or diced cheddar cheese
- 4 ounces of shredded or diced Monterey Jack cheese
- One tablespoon sugar
- 1 1/2 tsp salt
- Three cups bread flour
- One tablespoon butter at room temperature divided into opposite corners of the bread pan
- One teaspoon active dry yeast or bread machine yeast

Note: You can use any type of cheese or beer, and the beer does help with the bread's rising and overall texture and taste.

DIRECTIONS

1. On top of the cooker or in the microwave, heat the beer and cheese. There's no need to melt the cheese. Remove to mix and pour the mixture into the bread pan.
2. Let it cool again down to 110 ° F/43 ° C.
3. In the order specified in the recipe, add the remaining ingredients unless your manufacturer suggests a different order.
4. Select a simple white, 11.5-pound loaf, and medium crust framework press start.
5. Remove the loaf from the bread pan when done, and let it cool on the rack, and serve.

Nutritions *(Per serving):*

Calories: 265 kcal
Protein: 4.70 g

Fat: 12.52 g
Carbohydrates: 23.61 g

77. MOZZARELLA CHEESE AND PEPPERONI BREAD

PREPARATION: 10 MIN	**COOKING:** 2-4 H	**SERVES:** 13

INGREDIENTS

- 1 cup water + 2 tablespoons (110 ° F/43 ° C)
- Half cup medium shredded mozzarella cheese
- Two tablespoons sugar
- 1 1/2teaspoons garlic salt
- 1 1/2teaspoons dried oregano
- 3 1/4 cups bread flour
- 1 1/2teaspoons active dry yeast or bread machine yeast
- 2/3 cup pepperoni (1/4 inch or 1/2 centimeter)

DIRECTIONS

1. Place the ingredients in the bread pan in the sequence indicated above.
2. Choose the setting for white bread, 1.5-pound loaf, and medium crust.
3. Add in the diced pepperoni at the beep after the first kneading process after baking, let cool, slice, and serve.

Nutritions *(Per serving):*

Calories: 254 kcal
Protein: 4.32 g

Fat: 11.62 g
Carbohydrates: 22.61 g

CHAPTER 9
Vegetables and Fruit Bread

78. SUN VEGETABLE BREAD

PREPARATION: 15 MIN	**COOKING:** 3 H 45	**SERVES:** 8

INGREDIENTS

- 2 cups (250g) wheat flour
- 2 cups (250g) whole-wheat flour
- 2 teaspoons Panifarin
- 2 teaspoons yeast
- 1½ teaspoons salt
- 1 tablespoon sugar
- 1 tablespoon paprika dried slices
- 2 tablespoons dried beets
- 1 tablespoon dried garlic
- 1½ cups water
- 1 tablespoon vegetable oil

DIRECTIONS

1. Set the baking program, which should be 4 hours; crust color is Medium.
2. Be sure to look at the kneading phase of the dough to get a smooth and soft bun.

Nutritions *(Per serving):*

Calories: 253 kcal
Total Fat: 2.6 g
Cholesterol: 0 g

Sodium: 444 mg
Carbohydrates: 49.6 g
Fiber: 2.6 g

Sugar: 0.6 g
Protein: 7.2 g

79. TOMATO ONION BREAD

PREPARATION: 10 MIN	**COOKING:** 3 H 50	**SERVES:** 12

INGREDIENTS

- 2 cups all-purpose flour
- 1 cup wholemeal flour
- ½ cup warm water
- 4 3/4 ounces (140 ml) milk
- 3 tablespoons olive oil
- 2 tablespoons sugar
- 1 teaspoon salt
- 2 teaspoons dry yeast
- ½ teaspoon baking powder
- 5 sun-dried tomatoes
- 1 onion
- ¼ teaspoon black pepper

DIRECTIONS

1. Prepare all the necessary products. Finely chop the onion and sauté in a frying pan. Cut up the sun-dried tomatoes (10 halves).
2. Pour all liquid ingredients into the bowl, then cover with flour and put in the tomatoes and onions. Pour in the yeast and baking powder without touching the liquid.
3. Select the baking mode and start. You can choose the Bread with Additives program, and then the bread maker will knead the dough at low speeds.

Nutritions *(Per serving):*

Calories: 241 kcal
Fat: 6.4 g
Cholesterol: 1 g

Sodium: 305 mg
Carbohydrates: 40 g
Fiber: 3.5 g

Sugar: 6.8 g
Protein: 6.7 g

80. TOMATO BREAD

PREPARATION: 5 MIN	**COOKING:** 3 H 30	**SERVES:** 8

INGREDIENTS

- 3 tablespoons tomato paste
- 1½ cups (340 ml) water
- 4 1/3 cups (560g) flour
- 1½ tablespoon vegetable oil
- 2 teaspoons sugar
- 2 teaspoons salt
- 1 ½ teaspoons dry yeast
- ½ teaspoon oregano, dried
- ½ teaspoon ground sweet paprika

DIRECTIONS

1. Dilute the tomato paste in warm water. If you do not like the tomato flavor, reduce the amount of tomato paste, but putting less than 1 tablespoon does not make sense because the color will fade.
2. Prepare the spices. I added a little more oregano and Provencal herbs to the oregano and paprika (this bread also begs for spices).
3. Sieve the flour to enrich it with oxygen. Add the spices to the flour and mix well.
4. Pour the vegetable oil into the bread maker container. Add the tomato/water mixture, sugar, salt, the flour with spices, and then the yeast.
5. Turn on the bread maker (the Basic program—White Bread—the crust Medium).
6. After the end of the baking cycle, turn off the bread maker. Remove the bread container and take out the hot bread. Place it on the grate for cooling for 1 hour.

Nutritions *(Per serving):*

Calories: 281 kcal
Fat: 3.3 g
Cholesterol: 0 g

Sodium: 590 mg
Carbohydrates: 54.3 g
Fiber: 2.4 g

Sugar: 1.9 g
Protein: 7.6 g

81. CURD ONION BREAD WITH SESAME SEEDS

PREPARATION: 10 MIN   **COOKING:** 3 H 50 MIN   **SERVES:** 8

INGREDIENTS

- 3/4 cup water
- 3 2/3 cups wheat flour
- 3/4 cup cottage cheese
- 2 tablespoons softened butter
- 2 tablespoon sugar
- 1 ½ teaspoons salt
- 1 ½ tablespoon sesame seeds
- 2 tablespoons dried onions
- 1 ¼ teaspoons dry yeast

DIRECTIONS

1. Put the products in the bread maker according to its instructions.
2. Bake on the BASIC program.

Nutritions *(Per serving):*

Calories: 277 kcal
Fat: 4.7 g
Cholesterol: 9 g

Sodium: 547 mg
Carbohydrates: 48.4 g
Fiber: 1.9 g

Sugar: 3.3 g
Protein: 9.4 g

82. SQUASH CARROT BREAD

PREPARATION: 15 MIN   **COOKING:** 3 H 45 MIN   **SERVES:** 8

INGREDIENTS

- 1 small zucchini
- 1 baby carrot
- 1 cup whey
- 1 ½ cups (180g) white wheat flour
- 3/4 cup (100g) whole wheat flour
- 3/4 cup (100g) rye flour
- 2 tablespoons vegetable oil
- 1 teaspoon yeast, fresh
- 1 teaspoon salt
- ½ teaspoon sugar

DIRECTIONS

1. Cut/dice carrots and zucchini to about 8-10 mm (1/2 inch) in size.
2. In a frying pan, warm the vegetable oil and fry the vegetables over medium heat until soft. If desired, season the vegetables with salt and pepper.
3. Transfer the vegetables to a flat plate so that they cool down more quickly. While still hot, they cannot be added to the dough.
4. Now dissolve the yeast in the serum.
5. Send all kinds of flour, serum with yeast, salt, and sugar to the bakery.
6. Knead the dough in the Dough for the Rolls program.
7. At the very end of the batch, add the vegetables to the dough.
8. After adding vegetables, the dough will become moister. After the fermentation process, which will last about an hour before doubling the dough's volume, shift it onto a thickly floured surface.
9. Turn into a loaf and put it in an oiled form.
10. Conceal the form using a food film and leave for 1 to 1 1/3 hours.
11. Preheat oven to 450°F and put bread in it.
12. Bake the bread for 15 minutes, and then gently remove it from the mold. Lay it on the grate and bake for 15-20 minutes more

Nutritions *(Per serving):*

Calories: 220 kcal
Fat: 4.3 g
Cholesterol: 0 g

Sodium: 313 mg
Carbohydrates: 39.1 g
Fiber: 4.1 g

Sugar: 2.7 g
Protein: 6.6 g

83. BANANA BREAD

PREPARATION: 1 H 40	**COOKING:** 45 MIN	**SERVES:** 8

INGREDIENTS

- 1 teaspoon Baking powder
- 1/2 teaspoon Baking soda
- 2 bananas, peeled and halved lengthwise
- 2 cups all-purpose flour
- 2 eggs
- 3 tablespoon Vegetable oil
- 3/4 cup white sugar

DIRECTIONS

1. Put Ingredients in the bread pan. Select dough setting. Start and mix for about 3-5 minutes.
2. After 3-5 minutes, press stop. Do not continue to mix. Smooth out the top of the dough
3. Using the spatula and then select bake, start and bake for about 50 minutes. After 50 minutes, insert a toothpick into the top center to test doneness.
4. Test the loaf again. When the bread is completely baked, remove the pan from the machine and let the bread remain in the pan for10 minutes. Remove bread and cool in the wire rack.

Nutritions *(Per serving):*

Calories: 310 kcal
Carbohydrates: 40 g

Fat: 13 g
Protein: 3 g

84. BLUEBERRY BREAD

PREPARATION: 3 H 15　　**COOKING:** 45 MIN　　**SERVES:** 16

INGREDIENTS

- 1 1/8 to 1¼ cups water
- 6 ounces cream cheese, softened
- 2 tablespoons butter or margarine
- ¼ cup sugar
- 2 teaspoons salt
- 4½ cups bread flour
- 1½ teaspoons grated lemon peel
- 2 teaspoons cardamom
- 2 tablespoons non-fat: dry milk
- 2½ teaspoons red star brand active dry yeast
- 2/3 cup dried blueberries

DIRECTIONS

1. Place all ingredients except dried blueberries in the bread pan, using the least amount of liquid listed in the recipe. Select the light crust setting and the raisin/nut cycle. Press the start button.
2. Watch the dough as you knead. After 5 to 10 minutes, if it is dry and hard or if the machine seems to strain to knead it, add more liquid 1 tablespoon at a time until the dough forms a ball that is soft, tender, and slightly sticky to the touch.
3. When stimulated, add dried cranberries.
4. After the bake cycle is complete, remove the bread from the pan, place it on the cake, and allow it to cool.

Nutritions *(Per serving):*

Calories: 180 kcal　　　　　Fat: 3 g
Carbohydrates: 250 g　　　Protein: 9 g

85. ORANGE AND WALNUT BREAD

PREPARATION: 2 H 50   **COOKING:** 45 MIN   **SERVES:** 15

INGREDIENTS

- 1 egg white
- 1 tablespoon water
- ½ cup warm whey
- 1 tablespoons yeast
- 4 tablespoons sugar
- 2 oranges, crushed
- 4 cups flour
- 1 teaspoon salt
- 1 and ½ tablespoon salt
- 3 teaspoons orange peel
- 1/3 teaspoon vanilla
- 3 tablespoons walnut and almonds, crushed
- Crushed pepper, salt, cheese for garnish

DIRECTIONS

1. Add all the ingredients to your Bread Machine (except egg white, 1 tablespoon water, and crushed pepper/ cheese).
2. Set the program to the "Dough" cycle and let the cycle run.
3. Remove the dough (using lightly floured hands) and carefully place it on a floured surface.
4. Cover with a light film/cling paper and let the dough rise for 10 minutes.
5. Divide the dough into thirds after it has risen
6. Place on a lightly floured surface, roll each portion into 14x10 inch sized rectangles
7. Use a sharp knife to cut carefully cut the dough into strips of ½ inch width
8. Pick 2-3 strips and twist them multiple times, making sure to press the ends together
9. Preheat your oven to 400 degrees F
10. Take a bowl and stir egg white, water, and brush onto the breadsticks
11. Sprinkle salt, pepper/ cheese
12. Bake for 10-12 minutes until golden brown
13. Remove from the pan and place on a cooling rack. Serve and enjoy!

Nutritions *(Per serving):*

Calories: 437 kcal   Fat: 7 g   Sugar: 34 g

Carbohydrates: 82 g   Protein: 12 g   Fiber: 1 g

86. LEMON AND POPPY BUNS

PREPARATION: 2 H 50   **COOKING:** 45 MIN   **SERVES:** 10-20 BUNS

INGREDIENTS

- Melted Butter for grease
- 1 and 1/3 cups hot water
- 3 tablespoons powdered milk
- 2 tablespoons Crisco shortening
- 1 and ½ teaspoon salt
- 1 tablespoon lemon juice
- 4 and ¼ cups bread flour
- ½ teaspoon nutmeg
- 2 teaspoons grated lemon rind
- 2 tablespoons poppy seeds
- 1 and ¼ teaspoons yeast
- 2 teaspoons wheat gluten

DIRECTIONS

1. Add all the ingredients to your Bread Machine (except melted butter).
2. Set the program to the "Dough" cycle and let the cycle run.
3. Remove the dough (using lightly floured hands) and carefully place it on a floured surface.
4. Cover with a light film/cling paper and let the dough rise for 10 minutes.
5. Grease a large cookie sheet with butter.
6. Cut the risen dough into 15-20 pieces and shape them into balls.
7. Place the balls onto the sheet (2 inches apart) and cover.
8. Place in a warm place and let them rise for 30-40 minutes until the dough doubles.
9. Heat your oven to 375 degrees F, transfer the cookie sheet to your oven and bake for 12-15 minutes. Brush the top with a bit of butter, enjoy!

Nutritions *(Per serving):*

Calories: 231 kcal
Carbohydrates: 31 g

Fat: 11 g
Protein: 4 g

Sugar: 12 g
Fiber: 1 g

87. OLIVE BREAD FOR THE BREAD MACHINE

PREPARATION: 10 MIN   **COOKING:** 2-4 H   **SERVES:** 12

INGREDIENTS

- 1 cup plus 2 tablespoon water
- 1 tbsp vegetable oil
- 3 cups bread flour
- 2 tbsp sugar
- 1 tsp salt
- 1 1/4 tbsp bread maker yeast
- 3/4 cup olive, pitted and roughly chopped

DIRECTIONS

1. Put the ingredients, except for olives, in the bread pan, as suggested by your device's manufacturer.
2. Process it in the appropriate phase.
3. Add olives to the raisin/nut signal, or 5 to 10 minutes before the last kneading cycle ends prefer the dough process
4. Form the dough into 2 loaves and let it rise for 30 minutes.
5. Bake for 30 minutes in a preheated 375-degree oven.

VEGAN

Nutritions *(Per serving):*

Calories: 121 kcal
Protein: 5.44 g

Fat: 1.1 g
Carbohydrates: 22.39 g

88. BREAD MACHINE PUMPKIN YEAST BREAD

PREPARATION: 5 MIN | **COOKING:** 3 H | **SERVES:** 16

INGREDIENTS

- 1/2 cup plus 2 teaspoons milk (5 ounces)
- 1 cup mashed pumpkin (or canned pumpkin puree)
- 4 cups bread flour
- 2 tbsp vegetable oil
- 2 tbsp sugar
- 1 1/4 tsp salt
- 2 1/4 tsp active or instant dry yeast

DIRECTIONS

1. Add all the ingredients according to your bread machine supplier's suggested order, the default being the order listed in the list of ingredients above.
2. Opt for the setting on white bread, soft crust.
3. Instead, use 3 teaspoons of instant / rapid yeast and pick medium crust if you want to use the fast cycle on your bread machine.
4. Let your device do its thing and take pleasure in the loaf when it is done.

Nutritions *(Per serving):*

Calories: 153 kcal
Protein: 2.47 g

Fat: 6.33 g
Carbohydrates: 21.97 g

89. BREAD MAKER KALAMATA OLIVE BREAD

PREPARATION: 10 MIN   **COOKING:** 2 H   **SERVES:** 10

INGREDIENTS

- Olive brine: 1/3 - 1/2 cup
- Warm water: 1 cup (when with brine mixed sufficiently to produce 1 ½ cups)
- Olive oil: 2 tbsp
- Bread flour: 3 cups
- Whole wheat flour: 1 2/3 cup
- Salt: 1 1/2 tsp
- Sugar: 2 tbsp
- The dried leaf of basil: 1 1/2 tsp
- Active dry yeast: 2 tsp
- Olives: 1/2 to 2/3 cup (chopped Kalamata, approximately pitted olives about 2 dozen)

DIRECTIONS

1. Olive brine is put around a measure of 2 cups; slightly warm water is added to create 1 and a half cup amount.
2. Put everything in the bread machine, excluding olives, in keeping with your maker's desired order.
3. Choose on your bread maker the simple or wheat setup.
4. Add olives on the sound of beep that indicates the addition of ingredients that are mixed in.
5. Take a slice of it and eat it with butter or olive oil when the loaf is done baking.

Nutritions *(Per serving):*

Calories: 124 kcal
Protein: 2.46 g

Fat: 6.10 g
Carbohydrates: 20.96 g

90. AMAZING BREAD MACHINE "PULP" BREAD

PREPARATION: 15 MIN	**COOKING:** 2-4 H	**SERVES:** 12

INGREDIENTS

- 500 grams of all-purpose (about 2 1\2 cups) or bread flour.
- Veggie pulp or fruits: 1 1\2-2 cups (use organic apricots, peeled apples, peeled carrots, and organic peaches, add whatever you want)
- Dry yeast: 1 pkg
- Honey: 3 tbsp
- Salt: 1 Tbsp
- Vanilla: 1 tsp
- Water: 200 milliliters (7 oz)
- Olive oil: 1 tbsp

DIRECTIONS

1. In a container, mix your flour and yeast. Add the salt.
2. Next, place the pulp in a separate bowl, add the vanilla and honey. Blend well.
3. Add the water, followed by the oil, flour mixture, and finally, the pulp mixture into the bread machine baking pan. Set the machine to the quick cycle. Just pick a cycle that bakes for no more than 1 hour and 45 min, and it's done.

Nutritions *(Per serving):*

Calories: 132 kcal
Protein: 2.31 g

Fat: 6.25 g
Carbohydrates: 20.82 g

91. BREAD MACHINE CRANBERRY CORNMEAL BREAD

PREPARATION: 10 MIN	**COOKING:** 3 H 40 MIN	**SERVES:** 12

INGREDIENTS

- 1 cup plus 1 tablespoon water
- 3 tablespoons molasses or honey
- 2 tablespoons butter or margarine, softened
- 3 cups bread flour
- 1/3 cup cornmeal
- 1 1/2 teaspoons salt
- 2 teaspoons bread maker yeast
- 1/2 cup dried cranberries

DIRECTIONS

1. Weigh carefully, putting all ingredients except cranberries in the bread machine pan in the manufacturer's suggested order. At the Raisin / Nut signal, add cranberries, or 5 to 10 minutes before the last kneading process finishes.
2. Choose Cycle Basic / White. Using the Medium or Thin color Crust. Don't use cycles for the delay. Take the baked bread from the pan and cool it on the rack.

Nutritions *(Per serving):*

Calories: 185 kcal
Protein: 3.04 g

Fat: 8.82 g
Carbohydrates: 24.16 g

92. BREAD MACHINE BANANA OATMEAL BREAD

PREPARATION: 10 MIN	**COOKING:** 1-2 H	**SERVES:** 16

INGREDIENTS

- 2 teaspoons active dry yeast
- 1 cup oats
- 2 cups bread flour
- 1 cup whole wheat flour
- 1 tablespoon butter
- 1 tablespoon dry milk powder
- 1/2 teaspoon cinnamon
- 1/4 teaspoon nutmeg
- 2 tablespoons honey
- 1 teaspoon salt
- 1 egg
- 1/4 cup sour cream
- 2 cups chopped, ripe banana

DIRECTIONS

1. Add all ingredients to the machine, as suggested by the manufacturer.
2. Use the setting of "whole wheat" bread, the medium color of the crust.

Nutritions *(Per serving):*

Calories: 166 kcal
Protein: 2.19 g

Fat: 5.36 g
Carbohydrates: 27.85 g

93. BREAD MACHINE CRANBERRY CINNAMON BREAD

PREPARATION: 10 MIN | **COOKING:** 1-2 H | **SERVES:** 16

INGREDIENTS

- 1/2 tablespoon yeast
- 2 1/4 cups bread flour
- 1 tablespoon sugar
- 1 tablespoon shredded lemon or orange peel
- 1 tablespoon powdered milk
- 1/2 tablespoon salt
- 1 tablespoon ground cinnamon
- 1 tablespoon oil
- 1 1/8 cup water, warm
- 1 cup fresh or frozen cranberry

DIRECTIONS

1. Bring ingredients except for cranberries to room temperature and add to the machine, in order. Set the control darkness to 10 a.m. Click "the white bread" and press Start.
2. Thaw the cranberries. Add cranberries at the beep, 88 minutes to complete the cycle.

Nutritions *(Per serving):*

Calories: 170 kcal
Protein: 2.20 g

Fat: 5.41 g
Carbohydrates: 27.62 g

94. BREAD MACHINE APPLE OATMEAL BREAD WITH RAISINS

PREPARATION: 10 MIN | **COOKING:** 2-5 H | **SERVES:** 16

INGREDIENTS

- 1/2 cup old- fashioned rolled oats
- 2/3 cup warm water
- 1/2 cup unsweetened applesauce
- 2 3/4 cup bread flour
- 1 1/2 tsp salt
- 2 tbsp brown sugar
- 1 1/2 tablespoon non-fat dry milk powder
- 1 1/2 tbsp butter or margarine
- 1/3 of cup raisins
- 1 tsp ground cinnamon
- 2 tsp active dry yeast

DIRECTIONS

1. Combine all ingredients in the bread machine
2. Set the machine to a light crust and normal/white bread.
3. Remove the bread from the pan once the baking process is complete and let it cool down to room temperature on a wire rack for 1 hour before cutting into slices.
4. Store the bread until one week in an air-tight container.

Nutritions *(Per serving):*

Calories: 181 kcal
Protein: 2.98 g

Fat: 8.65 g
Carbohydrates: 23.69 g

95. BREAD MAKER PUMPKIN BREAD CINNAMON SWIRL

PREPARATION: 15 MIN   **COOKING:** 2-4 H   **SERVES:** 12

INGREDIENTS

- Pumpkin puree: 3/4 cup canned room temp
- Warm water: 1/4 cup
- Microwave warm milk for 20 sec: 1/3 cup
- Vegetable oil: 1 Tbsp.
- lightly packed brown sugar: 1/4 cup
- Salt: 1 tsp.
- Nutmeg: 1/4 tsp.
- Cinnamon: 1/2 tsp.
- lightly beaten egg: 1
- Bread flour: 3 cups approximately.
- Instant yeast Cinnamon Sugar Swirl: 3/4 Tbsp.
- Melted butter: 1 1/2 Tbsp.
- Light brown sugar: 1/2 cup combined with Cinnamon: 2 tsp.

Nutritions *(Per serving):*

Calories: 124 kcal
Protein: 5.30 g

DIRECTIONS

1. In the supplier suggested order, ingredients should be added to the bread machine.
2. To the bread machine pan, add pumpkin, hot milk water, vegetable oil, salt, egg, nutmeg, brown sugar, and cinnamon. Stir in flour. A well is created in the floured rim, and instant yeast is added to it. The dough cycle is turned over to the bread machine and allow it to do all the work. At first, when it's mixing, you'll test it, so you make sure the required flour. Slightly sticky will be the dough, but it should stay in a ball when the bread maker mixes. If very sticky is your dough, add some more flour, but do not overdo it.
3. When the process of dough is over, and there is a bread rise, the dough is punched down and remove from the pan. On a floured counter, the kneading of dough is done and starts to knead for some time to release the bubbles of air. Stretch the dough out to a rectangle of 9 "x22.' Brush the top with butter that is melted and sprinkle it with a mixture of sugar and cinnamon, leaving a border around the rim (1/2 inch)
4. Roll up tightly the dough, starting with the short end and then pinch to seal together. Put in a greased bread pan 9"x5"; cover with a kitchen towel and let it rise to almost double. 375 ° C oven is preheated and bake it for 30 minutes. The last 10 min, to prevent too much browning of the crust, tent it with foil. When it is finished, it will sound hollow when the bread is hit. A Sharp knife around the pan's border is run when the baking is done. Cooling is done by removing the bread. Slice, and have pleasure.

Fat: 1.2 g
Carbohydrates: 22.26 g

96. APPLE PIE BREAD

PREPARATION: 10 MIN	**COOKING:** 2-4 H	**SERVES:** 12

INGREDIENTS

- 1 cup buttermilk or soured milk
- 1/4 cup concentrate of apple juice
- 1 1/2 tbsp. Butter unsalted,
- 3 tbsp. Packed brown sugar
- 1 1/2 Tsp. Ground cinnamon
- 1 cup peeled and chopped gala apples
- 1 tsp. Salt
- 3 1/2 cups Bread flour NOT entire-purpose flour
- 4 tsp. vitally essential gluten from wheat
- 2 tsp. Dry bread yeast

DIRECTIONS

1. Put ingredients in the pan of the bread machine in the sequence pointed out above.
2. Choose a Sweet or simple setting and start the device.
3. After finishing, allow the bread to cool for about 15 minutes.
4. Brush with butter over the top and sides of the bread to prevent the crusts from hardening.
5. Enable the bread to cool longer than 15 minutes before cutting into slices.
6. The machine allows one (2 pounds) loaf or 10-large slices.

Notes: There are no preservatives in homemade bread, so it needs to be refrigerated after 2 days. Weigh milk in a measuring cup to make sure the milk is sour. Add 1 or 2 tablespoons of vinegar. Let the milk to curdle for about five minutes to sit out on the counter. Use the recipe above as a substitute for buttermilk. Entire-purpose flour does not contain the gluten required to tie together the ingredients and the bread flour. The bread might turn out crumbly. Use bread flour for better results.

Nutritions *(Per serving):*

Calories: 124 kcal
Protein: 5.30 g

Fat: 1.2 g
Carbohydrates: 22.26 g

97. BREAD MACHINE BANANA AMARANTH BREAD

PREPARATION: 10 MIN **COOKING:** 1-2 H **SERVES:** 16

INGREDIENTS

- 3/4 cup milk
- 1/3 cup mashed bananas
- 1 egg
- 3 tablespoons honey
- 1/3 teaspoon salt
- 1/4 teaspoon cinnamon
- 2 tablespoons essential gluten (optional)
- 1/3 cup amaranth flour
- 3 1/3 cups whole wheat flour
- 2 teaspoons yeast
- 1/3 cup chopped nuts (optional)

DIRECTIONS

1. Add ingredients (excluding nuts) to the bread pan, as instructed by the manufacturer.
2. Add nuts at the beep or just before final kneading. Use the whole wheat setting.

Nutritions *(Per serving):*

Calories: 177 kcal
Protein: 2.92 g

Fat: 8.48 g
Carbohydrates: 23.22 g

98. WREATH PUMPKIN BREAD

PREPARATION: 15 MIN | **COOKING:** 2-4 H | **SERVES:** 8

INGREDIENTS

- Pureed pumpkin: 3/4 cup
- Beaten egg: 1
- Milk: 1/2 cup
- Lukewarm water (105 ° to 115 ° F): 1/4 cup
- Sugar: 1/4 cup
- Melted butter: 1/4 cup
- Salt: 1 1/2 tsp
- Cinnamon: 1/2 tsp
- Nutmeg: 1/4 tsp
- Flour: 5 cups
- Bread maker yeast: 2 1/4 tsp
- Egg white: 1 big
- Pumpkin seeds: 1/4 cup
- Coarse sea salt

DIRECTIONS

1. Combine the pumpkin, egg, milk, water, sugar, butter, salt, cinnamon, and nutmeg in a big pot. Pour into the bread maker's pan.
2. Add flour to the pan. Sprinkle with leaven over the flour.
3. Proceed the Dough cycle in the bread maker.
4. Line a parchment-paper baking sheet. Remove bread maker dough and put it on a lined baking sheet.
5. Use thumbs to draw a hole in the middle of the dough, extend the dough to form a ring with a middle hole of around 5 inches in diameter.
6. Let the dough rise, around 1 hour, till the size is doubled.
7. Preheat the oven to 375 ° F.
8. Hold kitchen shears at an angle of 45 degrees, cut from the top of the ring to make 8 even cuts around the rim. To build the leaf form, pull the parts away from the center.
9. Beat the egg white and the water in a small bowl until it is foamy.
10. Sprinkle with pumpkin seeds and sea salt. Spray dough wreath with egg white mixture (may not use all of it).
11. Bake the loaf of bread for 25 to 30 minutes, or until golden brown. Cool on wire rack parchment.

Nutritions *(Per serving):*

Calories: 147 kcal
Protein: 2.37 g

Fat: 6.09 g
Carbohydrates: 21.11 g

99. GOLDEN EGG BREAD WITH DRIED FRUIT

PREPARATION: 2 H 45   **COOKING:** 30 MIN   **SERVES:** 12

INGREDIENTS

- 3/4 cup water
- 2 eggs
- 6 tbsp maize oil
- 1/4 cup sugar
- 1 1/2 tsp salt
- 2/3 cups dried cranberries, dried cherries, or raisins
- 3 cups bread flour
- 2 1/4 tsp instant bread maker yeast or 1/4-ounce pkg of active dry yeast

DIRECTIONS

1. Place ingredients in order given in the bread machine pan. (Add in the fruits at the end of the kneading process if desired) pour in an additional tablespoon of flour at a time to make the dough thick enough to form a ball and barely clean the edges.
2. Set machine on the cycle of dough. The dough will be doubled when complete. If not, let it keep on rising.
3. For the short dimension slightly longer than the pan, detach from the pan and roll into rectangle form. Roll the dough with the hands into a cylinder shape starting from the long side. Tuck ends underneath and through the roll carefully in a loaf pan with 9 x 4 inches. Cover with a clean towel loosely and permit to rise until almost double in a warm place. (May take an hour or longer)
4. Preheat oven to 350 ° C. Bake until golden brown and is cooked through and crust — approx. Just for 45 minutes. If required, cover with aluminum foil to protect from over-browning during the last third of the cooking time. Internal temperature, when finished, should reach 180-190 degrees. Place it on the shelf for 5 minutes before pan removal. Cool on a rack to cool off.

Nutritions *(Per serving):*

Calories: 146 kcal
Protein: 4.85 g

Fat: 3.06 g
Carbohydrates: 24.38 g

100. APPLE BUTTER BREAD

PREPARATION: 5 MIN	**COOKING:** 4 H	**SERVES:** 20

INGREDIENTS

- 1/3 cup Apple butter
- 2/3 cup milk
- 1/3 cup water
- 1 big egg
- 2 tbsp. unsalted butter
- 1 tbsp. Honey
- 4 cups bread flour do not use entire-purpose flour
- 1 tsp. Sea salt or salt
- 3/4 tsp. Allspice or apple pie sauce
- 2 tsp. Bread maker yeast
- 4 tsp. vital wheat gluten

DIRECTIONS

1. In the order given, layer in a canister of bread.
2. Place on the usual setting for bread.
3. It will take about 3 hours and 50 minutes.
4. Enable the bread to sit 15 minutes in the canister before removing it.
5. Butter tops and bread sides so as not to harden the crust.
6. Let the bread cool down for 15 minutes.
7. Slice in 20 half slices or 10 wide slices.

Notes: Check your yeast for the expiry date and make sure that it has not expired! There are no preservatives in the homemade bread, so it needs to be refrigerated after 2 days. Entire-purpose flour does not contain the gluten required to tie together the ingredients and the bread flour. The bread might turn out crumbly. Using bread flour for better results.

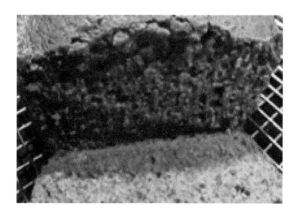

Nutritions *(Per serving):*

Calories: 181 kcal
Protein: 2.98 g

Fat: 8.65 g
Carbohydrates: 23.69 g

101. HONEY-SWEETENED RAISIN BREAD IN THE BREAD MACHINE

PREPARATION: 10 MIN   **COOKING:** 2 H 50 MIN   **SERVES:** 12

INGREDIENTS

- 1 cup raisins
- 1 cup milk or water
- 1 egg
- 2 tablespoons sunflower oil
- 2 tablespoons honey
- 3 cups whole wheat flour
- 1 tablespoon gluten
- 2 teaspoons ground cinnamon
- 1.5 teaspoons sea salt
- 2 teaspoons yeast

DIRECTIONS

1. In a small bowl, put the raisins, and add hot water to cover. Let them stand, drain, and set aside for 10 minutes.
2. Add all of the ingredients to your bread machine, as instructed by the manufacturer. Program the sweet and light settings, and start the machine.
3. When the machine beeps, add the raisins. A rubber spatula needs to be used to help them blend into the dough. Not all machines handle this part well. Unless you don't help them out, some raisins would be left on the pan's bottom.
4. After the baking process ends, remove the pan's bread and allow it to cool before slicing on a rack.

Nutritions *(Per serving):*

Calories: 140 kcal
Protein: 4.03 g

Fat: 2.24 g
Carbohydrates: 26.67 g

102. CARROT BREAD

PREPARATION: 30-45   **COOKING:** 2 H 10 MIN   **SERVES:** 12

INGREDIENTS

- 4 whole eggs
- ¼ teaspoon sea salt
- ½ cup (100 g, 4 oz) butter, melted
- ½ cup (120 g, 4 oz) brown sugar
- 1 tablespoon vanilla sugar
- 2 teaspoon ground cinnamon
- 3 cups (350 g, 13.50 oz) white bread flour
- 1 tablespoon baking powder
- ¼ cup (50 g) ground nuts
- ¾ cup (150 g) carrot, grated

DIRECTIONS

1. Prepare all of the ingredients for your bread and measuring means (a cup, a spoon, kitchen scales).
2. Carefully measure the ingredients into the pan, except the carrots and nuts.
3. Place all of the ingredients into the bread bucket in the right order, following the manual for your bread machine.
4. Close the cover.
5. Select the program of your bread machine to CAKE and choose the crust color to LIGHT.
6. Press START.
7. After the signal, put the grated carrots and nuts into the dough.
8. Wait until the program completes.
9. When done, take the bucket out and let it cool for 5-10 minutes.
10. Shake the loaf from the pan and let cool for 30 minutes on a cooling rack.
11. Cover the prepared bread with icing sugar.
12. Slice, serve and enjoy the taste of fragrant homemade bread.

Nutritions *(Per serving):*

Calories: 398 kcal
Fat: 17.3 g
Cholesterol: 112 mg

Sodium: 202 mg
Carbohydrates: 53 g
Fiber: 2.9 g

Protein: 9.2 g

103. SPINACH BREAD

PREPARATION: 30-45   **COOKING:** 3 H 30 MIN   **SERVES:** 20

INGREDIENTS

- 4 cups bread flour, sifted
- ½ cup frozen spinach
- 1 cup lukewarm water (80 degrees F)
- 1 tablespoon olive oil
- 1½ teaspoon active dry yeast

VEGAN

DIRECTIONS

1. Defrost the spinach.
2. Prepare all of the ingredients for your bread and measuring means (a cup, a spoon, kitchen scales).
3. Carefully measure the ingredients into the pan, except the spinach.
4. Place all of the ingredients into the bread bucket in the right order, following the manual for your bread machine.
5. Close the cover.
6. Select the program of your bread machine to BASIC and choose the crust color to MEDIUM.
7. Press START.
8. After the signal, put the spinach in the dough.
9. Wait until the program completes.
10. When done, take the bucket out and let it cool for 5-10 minutes.
11. Shake the loaf from the pan and let cool for 30 minutes on a cooling rack.
12. Slice, serve and enjoy the taste of fragrant homemade bread.

Nutritions *(Per serving):*

Calories: 238 kcal
Fat: 1.7 g

Carbohydrates: 44.4 g
Protein: 8.3 g

104. CHEESE BROCCOLI CAULIFLOWER BREAD

PREPARATION: 30MIN | **COOKING:** 3H 10 MIN | **SERVES:** 8

INGREDIENTS

- ¼ cup lukewarm water (80 degrees F)
- 4 tablespoons extra virgin olive oil
- 1 egg white
- 1 teaspoon fresh lemon juice
- 2/3 cup cheddar cheese, grated
- 3 tablespoons green onion
- ½ cup broccoli, chopped
- ½ cup cauliflower, chopped
- ½ teaspoon lemon pepper seasoning
- 2 cups bread flour
- 1 teaspoon active dry yeast

DIRECTIONS

1. Prepare all of the ingredients for your bread and measuring means (a cup, a spoon, kitchen scales).
2. Carefully measure the ingredients into the pan, except the vegetables and cheese.
3. Place all of the ingredients into the bread bucket in the right order, following the manual for your bread machine.
4. Close the cover.
5. Select the program of your bread machine to BASIC and choose the crust color to MEDIUM.
6. Press START.
7. After the signal, put the vegetables and cheese into the dough.
8. Wait until the program completes.
9. When done, take the bucket out and let it cool for 5-10 minutes.
10. Shake the loaf from the pan and let cool for 30 minutes on a cooling rack.
11. Slice, serve and enjoy the taste of fragrant homemade bread.

Nutritions *(Per serving):*

Calories: 220 kcal
Fat: 10.5 g

Carbohydrates: 25.2 g
Protein: 6.6 g

105. POTATO ROSEMARY BREAD

PREPARATION: 30MIN | **COOKING:** 30 MIN | **SERVES:** 16

INGREDIENTS

- 4 cups bread flour, sifted
- 1 tablespoon white sugar
- 1 tablespoon sunflower oil
- 1½ teaspoons salt
- 1½ cups lukewarm water
- 1 teaspoon active dry yeast
- 1 cup potatoes, mashed
- 2 teaspoons crushed rosemary

DIRECTIONS

1. Prepare all of the ingredients for your bread and measuring means (a cup, a spoon, kitchen scales).
2. Carefully measure the ingredients into the pan, except the potato and rosemary.
3. Place all of the ingredients into the bread bucket in the right order, following the manual for your bread machine.
4. Close the cover.
5. Select the program of your bread machine to BREAD with FILLINGS and choose the crust color to MEDIUM.
6. Press START.
7. After the signal, put the mashed potato and rosemary into the dough.
8. Wait until the program completes.
9. When done, take the bucket out and let it cool for 5-10 minutes.
10. Shake the loaf from the pan and let cool for 30 minutes on a cooling rack.
11. Slice, serve and enjoy the taste of fragrant homemade bread.

Nutritions *(Per serving):*

Calories: 106 kcal
Fat: 1 g

Carbohydrates: 21 g
Protein: 2.9 g

106. PARSLEY GARLIC BREAD

PREPARATION: 30MIN   **COOKING:** 30 MIN   **SERVES:** 16

INGREDIENTS

- 11/3 cups lukewarm milk
- 2 tablespoons unsalted butter, melted
- 4 teaspoons sugar
- 2 teaspoons table salt
- 22/3 teaspoons garlic powder
- 22/3 teaspoons fresh parsley, chopped
- 4 cups white bread flour
- 2¼ teaspoons bread machine yeast

DIRECTIONS

1. Decide the size of the loaf you want to make. Measure the ingredients.
2. Add the ingredients to the mold in the order described above.
3. Place the pan in the bread maker and close the cover.
4. Power up the bread machine. Choose the White/Basic setting, then the loaf size, and in conclusion, the crust color. Go ahead with the cycle.
5. Once the cycle is complete and the bread is cooked, gently remove the mold from the machine. Use a potholder because the handle is going to be hot. Allow sitting a few minutes.
6. Remove the loaf from the skillet and let cool on a wire rack for at least 10 minutes before slicing.

Nutritions *(Per serving):*

Calories: 143 kcal
Fat: 2.2 g

Carbohydrates: 24.6 g
Protein: 4.3 g

107. SWISS OLIVE BREAD

PREPARATION: 30MIN   **COOKING:** 30 MIN   **SERVES:** 16

INGREDIENTS

- 11/3 cup s lukewarm milk
- 2 tablespoons unsalted butter, melted
- 11/3 teaspoons minced garlic
- 2 tablespoons sugar
- 11/3 teaspoons table salt
- 1 cup Swiss cheese, shredded
- 4 cups white bread flour
- 1½ teaspoons bread machine yeast
- ½ cup chopped black olives

DIRECTIONS

1. Select the size of loaf you would like to make. Measure your ingredients.
2. Combine all of the ingredients except for the olives to the bread pan in the order listed above.
3. Place the pan in the bread machine and close the lid.
4. Turn on the bread maker. Select the White/Basic or Fruit/Nut (if your machine has this setting) setting, then the loaf size, and finally the crust color. Start the cycle.
5. Once the machine signals to add ingredients, add the olives. (Some machines have a fruit/nut hopper where you can add the olives when you start the machine. The machine will automatically add them to the dough during the baking process.)
6. When the cycle is finished, and the bread is baked, carefully remove the pan from the machine. Use a potholder as the handle will be very hot. Let rest for a few minutes.
7. Remove the bread from the pan and allow to cool on a wire rack for at least 10 minutes before slicing.

Nutritions *(Per serving):*

Calories: 147 kcal
Fat: 4.8 g

Carbohydrates: 26.7 g
Protein: 5.8 g

108. CHIVE AND DILL BREAD

PREPARATION: 10 MIN **COOKING:** 3 H **SERVES:** 16

INGREDIENTS

- 3/4 cup water (70° to 80°)
- 1/2 cup spreadable cream cheese chive and onion
- 2 tbsp sugar
- 2 tsp dill weed
- 1-1/4 tsp salt
- 3 cups all-purpose flour
- 1 package of yeast (active dry) (1/4 ounce)

DIRECTIONS

1. Combine all the bread ingredients in the bread maker manufacturer's suggested order in your bread machine pan.
2. Select basic bread setting with medium or light crust and loaf size. Close lid and press start.
3. Once it is about 5 minutes into the mixing, check and add about 1 to 2 tbsp water or more flour if needed.
4. Once done, remove bread from pan and let cool on a wire rack before slicing.

Nutritions *(Per serving):*

Calories: 121 kcal
Fat: 3 g

Carbohydrates: 20 g
Protein: 3 g

109. ROSEMARY GARLIC BREAD

PREPARATION: 10 MIN | **COOKING:** 3 H | **SERVES:** 6

INGREDIENTS

- 3 cups all-purpose flour
- 2 tsp crushed dried rosemary
- 1/2 tsp garlic powder
- 1/2 tsp ground thyme
- 3 tbsp olive oil
- 1 1/2 tsp salt
- 3 tbsp white sugar
- 2 1/2 tsp active dry yeast
- 1 cup warm water

DIRECTIONS

1. Combine all the bread ingredients in the bread maker manufacturer's suggested order in your bread machine pan.
2. Select the basic setting with medium or light crust and loaf size. Close lid and press start.
3. Once it is about 5 minutes into the mixing, check and add about 1 to 2 tbsp water or more flour if needed.
4. Once done, remove bread from pan and let cool on a wire rack before slicing.

Nutritions *(Per serving):*

Calories: 319 kcal
Fat: 7.5 g

Carbohydrates: 55 g
Protein: 7.2 g

110. BASIL HERBED BREAD

PREPARATION: 10 MIN | **COOKING:** 3 H | **SERVES:** 14

INGREDIENTS

- 2-1/4 teaspoons active dry yeast
- 3-1/2 cups bread flour
- 1/2 teaspoon dried thyme
- 3/4 teaspoon dried basil
- 1-1/2 teaspoons salt
- 1-1/2 teaspoons sugar
- 2 tablespoons mashed potato flakes
- 2 tablespoons dried minced onion
- 1 tablespoon butter, softened
- 1-1/2 cups water (70° to 80°)

DIRECTIONS

1. Combine all the bread ingredients in the bread maker manufacturer's suggested order in your bread machine pan.
2. Select the basic setting with medium or light crust and loaf size. Close lid and press start.
3. Once it is about 5 minutes into the mixing, check and add about 1 to 2 tbsp water or more flour if needed.
4. Once done, remove bread from pan and let cool on a wire rack before slicing.

Nutritions *(Per serving):*

Calories: 101 kcal
Fat: 1 g

Carbohydrates: 20 g
Protein: 4 g

111. OLIVE CHEDDAR BREAD

PREPARATION: 10 MIN | **COOKING:** 3 H | **SERVES:** 16

INGREDIENTS

- 3/4 cup pimiento-stuffed olives, drained thoroughly and sliced
- 2 tsp active dry yeast
- 3 cups bread flour
- 1-1/4 cups shredded sharp cheddar cheese
- 3/4 tsp salt
- 4 tsp sugar
- 1 cup water (70° to 80°)

DIRECTIONS

1. Combine all the bread ingredients in the order suggested by the manufacturer in the bread machine pan except olives.
2. Push the basic bread setting and the crust you want with loaf size.
3. Once it's about 5 minutes into the mixing, check and add about 1 to 2 tablespoons of water or more flour if needed.
4. Add the olives just 5 minutes before final kneading or at the raisin or nut sound. (Your machine may beep to notify you).
5. Withdraw bread from pan and let cool on a wire rack, slice with a sharp knife into slices.

Nutritions *(Per serving):*

Calories: 124 kcal
Fat: 4 g

Carbohydrates: 18 g
Protein: 5 g

112. HERB BREAD MACHINE BREAD

PREPARATION: 15 MIN | **COOKING:** 3H 40 MIN | **SERVES:** 16

INGREDIENTS

- 2-1/4 tsp active dry yeast
- 3 cups bread flour
- 1/2 tsp of garlic powder
- 1/2 tsp dried basil
- 1/2 tsp minced garlic
- 1 tsp salt
- 1 tbsp grated Parmesan cheese
- 1 tbsp softened butter
- 1-1/2 tsp sugar
- 1/4 cup warm sour cream (70° to 80°)
- 1/4 cup warm water (70° to 80°)
- 2/3 cup warm milk (70° to 80°)

DIRECTIONS

1. Place the ingredients in the bread machine pan in the order suggested by the manufacturer.
2. Push the basic bread setting and light crust with loaf size.
3. Once it is about 5 minutes into the mixing, check and add about 1 to 2 tablespoons of water or more flour if needed.
4. Once done, remove bread from pan and let cool on a wire rack before slicing.

Nutritions *(Per serving):*

Calories: 100 kcal
Fat: 2 g

Carbohydrates: 17 g
Protein: 4 g

113. CHILI BEER BREAD

PREPARATION: 5 MIN | **COOKING:** 3 H | **SERVES:** 10

INGREDIENTS

- 2 tsp active dry yeast
- 1/2 tsp salt
- 1/4 tsp garlic powder
- 1 tsp chili powder
- 1 tbsp dried minced onion
- 1/8 tsp ground cumin
- 2 1/4 cups bread flour
- 1 tbsp olive oil
- 1/4 tsp hot chile oil
- 1/4 tsp ground cayenne pepper
- 1 tsp beef bouillon
- 7/8 cup beer

DIRECTIONS

1. Combine all the bread ingredients in the bread maker manufacturer's suggested order in your bread machine pan.
2. Select the French bread or White Bread with loaf size. Close lid and press start.
3. Once it is 5 minutes into the mixing, check and add about 1 to 2 tbsp water or more flour if needed.
4. Once done, remove bread from pan and let cool on a wire rack before slicing.

Nutritions *(Per serving):*

Calories: 28 kcal
Fat: 1.6 g

Carbohydrates: 1.7 g
Protein: 0.5 g

114. OREGANO BASIL HERB BREAD

PREPARATION: 10 MIN   **COOKING:** 3 H   **SERVES:** 8

INGREDIENTS

- 2 tsp bread machine yeast
- 2 tbsp all-purpose flour
- 3 cups all-purpose flour
- 1 tsp dried basil
- 1 tsp dried oregano
- 2 tsp dried rosemary leaves, crushed
- 2 tbsp extra-virgin olive oil
- 2 tbsp white sugar
- 1 tsp salt
- 1 egg, beaten
- 1 cup warm water

DIRECTIONS

1. Combine all the bread ingredients in the bread maker manufacturer's suggested order in your bread machine pan.
2. Select the basic setting with a light crust and loaf size. Close lid and press start.
3. Once it is about 5 minutes into the mixing, check and add about 1 to 2 tbsp water or more flour if needed.
4. Once done, remove bread from pan and let cool on a wire rack before slicing.

Nutritions *(Per serving):*

Calories: 234 kcal   Carbohydrates: 41 g
Fat: 4.6 g   Protein: 6.3 g

115. ONION AND DILL HERB BREAD

PREPARATION: 10 MIN   **COOKING:** 3 H   **SERVES:** 8

INGREDIENTS

- 2 tsp bread machine yeast
- 2 tbsp all-purpose flour
- 3 cups all-purpose flour
- 1/4 cup finely chopped onion
- 1 tablespoon dried dill
- 2 tbsp extra-virgin olive oil
- 2 tbsp white sugar
- 1 tsp salt
- 1 egg, beaten
- 1 cup warm water

DIRECTIONS

1. Combine all the bread ingredients in the bread maker manufacturer's suggested order in your bread machine pan.
2. Select the basic setting with light crust with loaf size. Close lid and press start.
3. Once it is 5 minutes into the mixing, check and add about 1 to 2 tbsp water or more flour if needed.
4. Once done, remove bread from pan and let cool on a wire rack before slicing.

Nutritions *(Per serving):*

Calories: 234 kcal
Fat: 4.6 g

Carbohydrates: 41 g
Protein: 6.3 g

116. CARDAMOM HONEY BREAD

PREPARATION: 30MIN | **COOKING:** 30 MIN | **SERVES:** 16

INGREDIENTS

- 11/8 cups lukewarm milk
- 1 egg, at room temperature
- 2 teaspoons unsalted butter, melted
- ¼ cup honey
- 11/3 teaspoons table salt
- 4 cups white bread flour
- 11/3 teaspoons ground cardamom
- 12/3 teaspoons bread machine yeast

DIRECTIONS

1. Decide the size of loaf you would like to make. Measure the ingredients.
2. Add ingredients to mold in order as above.
3. Place the pan in the bread maker and close the cover.
4. Switch on the bread maker. Choose the White/Basic setting, then the loaf size, and in conclusion, the crust color. Begin the cycle.
5. Once the cycle is complete and the bread is cooked, gently remove the mold from the machine. Use a potholder as it will be very hot. Allow to sit a few minutes.
6. Remove the bread from the pan and allow to cool on a wire rack for at least 10 minutes before slicing.

Nutritions *(Per serving):*

Calories: 148 kcal
Fat: 2.2 g

Carbohydrates: 28.2 g
Protein: 4.8 g

CHAPTER 10
Herb and Spice Bread

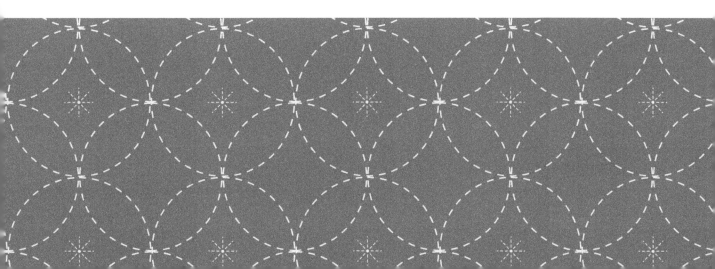

117. FRAGRANT HERB BREAD

PREPARATION: 10 MIN   **COOKING:** 1-4 H   **SERVES:** 8

INGREDIENTS

- ¾ cup water, at 80°F
- 1 tablespoon melted butter, cooled
- 1 tablespoon sugar
- ¾ teaspoon salt
- 2 tablespoons skim milk powder
- 1 teaspoon dried thyme
- 1 teaspoon dried chives
- ½ teaspoon dried oregano
- 2 cups white bread flour
- ¾ teaspoon bread machine yeast or instant yeast

DIRECTIONS

1. Put the ingredients in your bread machine as suggested by the manufacturer.
2. Set the machine to Basic/White bread, select a light or medium crust, then press Start.
3. Once the bread is finished, take the bucket out of the machine.
4. Chill the bread for 5 minutes.
5. Carefully shake the bucket to remove the loaf and turn it out onto a rack to cool.

Nutritions *(Per serving):*

Calories: 141 kcal
Fat: 2 g

Carbohydrates: 27 g
Protein: 4 g

118. ROSEMARY BREAD

PREPARATION: 10 MIN   **COOKING:** 2-4 H   **SERVES:** 8

INGREDIENTS

- ¾ cup plus 1 tablespoon water, at 80°F to 90°F
- 12/3 tablespoons melted butter, cooled
- 2 teaspoons sugar
- 1 teaspoon salt
- 1 tablespoon finely chopped fresh rosemary
- 2 cups white bread flour
- 11/3 teaspoons bread machine yeast or instant yeast

DIRECTIONS

1. Put the ingredients in your bread machine as suggested by the manufacturer.
2. Set the machine to Basic/White bread, select a light or medium crust, then press Start.
3. Once the bread is finished, take the bucket out of the machine.
4. Chill the bread for 5 minutes.
5. Carefully shake the bucket to remove the loaf and turn it out onto a rack to cool.

Ingredient tip: If you are not a fan of bits of chopped rosemary in your bread, try infusing the water in the recipe instead. Pour a little more than the required amount of water in a saucepan with the chopped rosemary. Simmer the liquid for at least 15 minutes, strain out the herbs, and cool the water to the correct bread-making temperature.

Nutritions *(Per serving):*

Calories: 142 kcal
Fat: 3 g

Carbohydrates: 25 g
Protein: 4 g

119. SPICY CAJUN BREAD

PREPARATION: 10 MIN	**COOKING:** 2-4 H	**SERVES:** 8

INGREDIENTS

- ¾ cup water, at 80°F
- 1 tablespoon melted butter, cooled
- 2 teaspoons tomato paste
- 1 tablespoon sugar
- 1 teaspoon salt
- 2 tablespoons skim milk powder
- ½ tablespoon Cajun seasoning
- 1/8 teaspoon onion powder
- 2 cups white bread flour
- 1 teaspoon bread machine yeast or instant yeast

DIRECTIONS

1. Put the ingredients in your bread machine according to the recommendations of the manufacturer.
2. Set the machine to Basic/White bread, select a light or medium crust, then press Start.
3. Once the bread is finished, take the bucket out of the machine.
4. Let the loaf cool for five minutes.
5. Carefully shake the bucket to remove the loaf and turn it out onto a rack to cool.

Tip: To ensure a uniform reddish tint in this bread, stir the tomato paste into the water before adding all the other ingredients.

Nutritions *(Per serving):*

Calories: 141 kcal
Fat: 2 g

Carbohydrates: 27 g
Protein: 4 g

120. AROMATIC LAVENDER BREAD

PREPARATION: 10 MIN   **COOKING:** 2-4 H   **SERVES:** 8

INGREDIENTS

- ¾ cup milk, at 80°F
- 1 tablespoon melted butter, cooled
- 1 tablespoon sugar
- ¾ teaspoon salt
- 1 teaspoon chopped fresh lavender flowers
- ¼ teaspoon lemon zest
- ¼ teaspoon chopped fresh thyme
- 2 cups white bread flour
- ¾ teaspoon bread machine yeast or instant yeast

DIRECTIONS

1. Put the ingredients in your bread machine as recommended by the manufacturer.
2. Set the machine to Basic/White bread, select a light or medium crust, then press Start.
3. Once the bread is finished, take the bucket out of the machine.
4. Let stand for 5 minutes.
5. Carefully shake the bucket to remove the loaf and turn it out onto a rack to cool.

Note: In the winter, when lavender flowers are scarce, substitute chopped fresh thyme because it has a similar flavor.

Nutritions *(Per serving):*

Calories: 144 kcal
Fat: 2 g

Carbohydrates: 27 g
Protein: 4 g

121. CRACKED BLACK PEPPER BREAD

PREPARATION: 10 MIN | **COOKING:** 2-4 H | **SERVES:** 8

INGREDIENTS

- ¾ cup water, at 80°F
- 1 tablespoon melted butter, cooled
- 1 tablespoon sugar
- ¾ teaspoon salt
- 2 tablespoons skim milk powder
- 1 tablespoon minced chives
- ½ teaspoon garlic powder
- ½ teaspoon cracked black pepper
- 2 cups white bread flour
- ¾ teaspoon bread machine yeast or instant yeast

DIRECTIONS

1. Put the ingredients in your bread machine according to the recommendations of the manufacturer.
2. Set the machine to Basic/White bread, select a light or medium crust, then press Start.
3. Once the bread is finished, take the bucket out of the machine.
4. Let stand for 5 minutes.
5. Carefully shake the bucket to remove the loaf and turn it out onto a rack to cool.

Tip: You can buy cracked black pepper in the supermarket in the spice aisle if you don't have the time or inclination to crack your own. This pepper product will not be as strong or as fresh, but you will still taste the bread's flavor kick.

Nutritions *(Per serving):*

Calories: 141 kcal
Fat: 2 g

Carbohydrates: 27 g
Protein: 4 g

122. HERB AND GARLIC CREAM CHEESE BREAD

PREPARATION: 10 MIN | **COOKING:** 2-4 H | **SERVES:** 8

INGREDIENTS

- 1/3 cup water, at 80°F
- 1/3 cup herb and garlic cream cheese, at room temperature
- 1 egg, at room temperature
- 4 teaspoons melted butter, cooled
- 1 tablespoon sugar
- 2/3 teaspoon salt
- 2 cups white bread flour
- 1 teaspoon bread machine yeast or instant yeast

DIRECTIONS

1. Put the ingredients in your bread machine according to the recommendations of the manufacturer.
2. Set the machine to Basic/White bread, select a light or medium crust, then press Start.
3. When the loaf is done, remove the bucket from the machine.
4. Let the loaf cool for 5 minutes.
5. Gently shake the bucket to remove the loaf and turn it out onto a rack to cool.
6. Note: Plain, garlic, or smoked salmon cream cheese would all be delightful choices in this recipe to create interesting varieties of bread. Do not use low-fat or nonfat products when making this loaf.

Nutritions *(Per serving):*

Calories: 182 kcal
Fat: 6 g

Carbohydrates: 27 g
Protein: 5 g

123. HONEY-SPICE EGG BREAD

PREPARATION: 10 MIN **COOKING:** 2-4 H **SERVES:** 8

INGREDIENTS

- ¾ cup milk, at 80°F
- 1 egg, at room temperature
- 1 tablespoon melted butter, cooled
- 4 teaspoons honey
- 2/3 teaspoon salt
- 2/3 teaspoon ground cinnamon
- 1/3 teaspoon ground cardamom
- 1/3 teaspoon ground nutmeg
- 2 cups white bread flour
- 11/3 teaspoons bread machine yeast or instant yeast

DIRECTIONS

1. Place the ingredients in your bread machine as recommended by the manufacturer.
2. Program the machine for Basic/White bread, select light or medium crust, and press Start.
3. When the loaf is done, remove the bucket from the machine.
4. Let the loaf cool for 5 minutes.
5. Gently shake the bucket to remove the loaf and turn it out onto a rack to cool.

Tip: Cardamom has a citrusy, almost smoky aroma and is a member of the ginger family. Most of the cardamom found in grocery stores is the ground-up black cardamom, which is less expensive than green cardamom, one of the world's most costly spices.

Nutritions *(Per serving):*

Calories: 162 kcal
Fat: 3 g

Carbohydrates: 28 g
Protein: 5 g

124. CINNAMON BREAD

PREPARATION: 10 MIN   **COOKING:** 2-4 H   **SERVES:** 8

INGREDIENTS

- 2/3 cup milk, at 80°F
- 1 egg, at room temperature
- 3 tablespoons melted butter, cooled
- 1/3 cup sugar
- 1/3 teaspoon salt
- 1 teaspoon ground cinnamon
- 2 cups white bread flour
- 11/3 teaspoons bread machine yeast or active dry yeast

DIRECTIONS

1. Combine the ingredients in your bread machine as recommended by the manufacturer.
2. Set the machine to Basic/White bread, select a light or medium crust, then press Start.
3. When the loaf is done, remove the bucket from the machine.
4. Let the loaf cool for 5 minutes.
5. Gently shake the bucket to remove the loaf and turn it out onto a rack to cool.

Note: Other warm spices, such as nutmeg or ginger, can also be added in pinches to the recipe to create a more complex flavor.

Nutritions *(Per serving):*

Calories: 198 kcal
Fat: 5 g

Carbohydrates: 34 g
Protein: 5 g

125. SIMPLE GARLIC BREAD

PREPARATION: 10 MIN | **COOKING:** 2-4 H | **SERVES:** 8

INGREDIENTS

- 2/3 cup milk, at 70°F to 80°F°
- 1 tablespoon melted butter, cooled
- 2 teaspoons sugar
- 1 teaspoon salt
- 11/3 teaspoons garlic powder
- 11/3 teaspoons chopped fresh parsley
- 2 cups white bread flour
- 11/8 teaspoons bread machine yeast or instant yeast

DIRECTIONS

1. Put the ingredients in your bread machine according to the recommendations of the manufacturer.
2. Set the machine to Basic/White bread, select a light or medium crust, then press Start.
3. When the loaf is done, remove the bucket from the machine.
4. Let the loaf cool for 5 minutes.
5. Gently shake the bucket to remove the loaf and turn it out onto a rack to cool.

Substitution tip: Minced garlic can be substituted for the garlic powder. Add the fresh garlic to the wet ingredients in the same amount as the powdered garlic.

Nutritions *(Per serving):*

Calories: 144 kcal
Fat: 2 g

Carbohydrates: 26 g
Protein: 4 g

126. HERBED PESTO BREAD

PREPARATION: 10 MIN   **COOKING:** 2-4 H   **SERVES:** 8

INGREDIENTS

- 2/3 cup water, at 80°F
- 1½ tablespoons melted butter, cooled
- 1 teaspoon minced garlic
- ½ tablespoon sugar
- ¾ teaspoon salt
- 2 tablespoons chopped fresh parsley
- ¾ teaspoon chopped fresh basil
- ¼ cup grated Parmesan cheese
- 2 cups white bread flour
- ¾ teaspoon bread machine or active dry yeast

DIRECTIONS

1. Put the ingredients in your bread machine as suggested by the manufacturer.
2. Set the machine to Basic/White bread, select a light or medium crust, then press Start.
3. When the bread has finished, remove the bucket from the machine.
4. Let the loaf cool for 5 minutes.
5. Gently shake the bucket to remove the loaf and turn it out onto a rack to cool.

Nutritions *(Per serving):*

Calories: 149 kcal
Fat: 3 g

Carbohydrates: 25 g
Protein: 5 g

127. CARAWAY RYE BREAD

PREPARATION: 10 MIN | **COOKING:** 2-4 H | **SERVES:** 12

INGREDIENTS

- 11/8 cups water, at 80°F
- 1¾ tablespoons melted butter, cooled
- 3 tablespoons dark brown sugar
- 1½ tablespoons dark molasses
- 11/8 teaspoons salt
- 1½ teaspoons caraway seed
- ¾ cup dark rye flour
- 2 cups white bread flour
- 11/8 teaspoons bread machine yeast or instant yeast

DIRECTIONS

1. Place the ingredients in your bread machine following the recommendations of the manufacturer.
2. Program the machine for Basic/White bread, select light or medium crust, and press Start.
3. When the loaf is done, remove the bucket from the machine.
4. Let the loaf cool for 5 minutes.
5. Gently shake the bucket to remove the loaf and turn it out onto a rack to cool.

Nutritions *(Per serving):*

Calories: 134 kcal
Fat: 2 g

Carbohydrates: 26 g
Protein: 4 g

128. ANISE LEMON BREAD

PREPARATION: 10 MIN   **COOKING:** 2-4 H   **SERVES:** 12

INGREDIENTS

- ¾ cup water, at 80°F
- 1 egg, at room temperature
- ¼ cup butter, melted and cooled
- ¼ cup honey
- ½ teaspoon salt
- 1 teaspoon anise seed
- 1 teaspoon lemon zest
- 3 cups white bread flour
- 2 teaspoons bread machine yeast or instant yeast

DIRECTIONS

1. Place the ingredients in your bread machine as suggested by the manufacturer.
2. Set the machine to Basic/White bread, select a light or medium crust, then press Start.
3. Once the bread is finished, take the bucket out of the machine.
4. Let the loaf cool for 5 minutes.
5. Gently shake the bucket to remove the loaf and turn it out onto a rack to cool.

Nutritions *(Per serving):*

Calories: 158 kcal
Fat: 5 g

Carbohydrates: 30 g
Protein: 4 g

129. FRAGRANT CARDAMOM BREAD

PREPARATION: 10 MIN | **COOKING:** 2-4 H | **SERVES:** 16

INGREDIENTS

- 1 cup plus 2 tablespoons milk, at 80°F to 90°F
- 1 egg, at room temperature
- 2 teaspoons melted butter, cooled
- ¼ cup honey
- 11/3 teaspoons salt
- 11/3 teaspoons ground cardamom
- 4 cups white bread flour
- 12/3 teaspoons bread machine yeast or instant yeast

DIRECTIONS

1. Place the ingredients in your bread machine as suggested by the manufacturer.
2. Set the machine to Basic/White bread, select a light or medium crust, then press Start.
3. When the bread has finished, remove the bucket from the machine.
4. Chill the bread for 5 minutes.
5. Carefully shake the bucket to remove the loaf and turn it out onto a rack to cool.

Ingredient tip: Three types of cardamom can be purchased for your recipe needs: green, black, and Madagascar. Ground cardamom is the most common product in mainstream grocery stores, and it is made from green cardamom. If you want a very intense flavor, buy this spice in the pods and grind it yourself.

Nutritions *(Per serving):*

Calories: 149 kcal
Fat: 2 g

Carbohydrates: 29 g
Protein: 5 g

130. CHOCOLATE MINT BREAD

PREPARATION: 10 MIN   **COOKING:** 2-4 H   **SERVES:** 16

INGREDIENTS

- 1¼ cups plus 2 tablespoons milk, at 80°F to 90°F
- ¼ teaspoon mint extract
- 2 tablespoons butter, melted and cooled
- 1/3 cup sugar
- 1¼ teaspoons salt
- 2 tablespoons unsweetened cocoa powder
- 4 cups white bread flour
- 2½ teaspoons bread machine or instant yeast
- ¾ cup semisweet chocolate chips

DIRECTIONS

1. Put the ingredients in your bread maker, as suggested by the manufacturer.
2. Program the machine for Sweet bread, select light or medium crust, and press Start.
3. When the loaf is baked, remove the bucket from the machine.
4. Allow the loaf to cool for 5 minutes.
5. Carefully shake the bucket to remove the loaf and turn it out onto a rack to cool.

Tip: Omit the cocoa powder and mint extract and use mint chocolate chips for delicious and different bread, or you can use all three ingredients to double up on the mint chocolate flavor.

Nutritions *(Per serving):*

Calories: 177 kcal
Fat: 3 g

Carbohydrates: 32 g
Protein: 4 g

131. MOLASSES CANDIED-GINGER BREAD

PREPARATION: 10 MIN | **COOKING:** 2-4 H | **SERVES:** 16

INGREDIENTS

- 11/3 cups milk, at 80°F
- 1 egg, at room temperature
- 1/3 cup dark molasses
- ¼ cup butter, melted and cooled
- 2/3 teaspoon salt
- 1/3 cup chopped candied ginger
- 2/3 cup quick oats
- 4 cups white bread flour
- 2½ teaspoons bread machine or instant yeast

DIRECTIONS

1. Place the ingredients in your bread machine according to the recommendations of the manufacturer.
2. Set the machine to Basic/White bread, select a light or medium crust, then press Start.
3. Once the bread is finished, take the bucket out of the machine.
4. Chill the bread for 5 minutes.
5. Carefully shake the bucket to remove the loaf and turn it out onto a rack to cool.

Ingredient tip: Making candied ginger at home is quite easy and requires very few ingredients or tools. Simply blanch peeled slices of ginger until they are tender, and then simmer the ginger in a syrup made from sugar of the same weight as the ginger and ¼ cup water. Simmer until the syrup is completely evaporated, and cool the candied ginger on a wire rack.

Nutritions *(Per serving):*

Calories: 191 kcal
Fat: 4 g

Carbohydrates: 32 g
Protein: 5 g

132. GARLIC, HERB, AND CHEESE BREAD

PREPARATION: 20MIN | **COOKING:** 1 H | **SERVES:** 12

INGREDIENTS

- 1/2 cup ghee
- 6 eggs
- 2 cups almond flour
- 1 tsp baking powder
- 1/2 tsp xanthan gum
- 1 cup cheddar cheese, shredded
- 1 tbsp garlic powder
- 1 tbsp parsley
- 1/2 tbsp oregano
- 1/2 tsp salt

DIRECTIONS

1. Lightly beat eggs and ghee before pouring into the bread machine pan.
2. Add the remaining ingredients to the pan.
3. Set bread machine to gluten-free.
4. When the bread is baked, remove the bread machine pan from the bread machine.
5. Let cool before transferring to a cooling rack.
6. You can store your bread for up to 5 days in the refrigerator.

Nutritions *(Per serving):*

Calories: 156 kcal
Carbohydrates: 4 g

Protein: 5 g
Fat: 13 g

133. MIXED HERBS BREAD

PREPARATION: 20MIN   **COOKING:** 1 H   **SERVES:** 6

INGREDIENTS

- 4 eggs
- 1/3 cup unsalted melted butter
- Almond flour, one and a half cup full
- Xanthan gum, half a teaspoon
- Salt, half a teaspoon
- Oregano, dried, half a teaspoon
- Dry basil, half a teaspoon
- Baking powder, one teaspoon
- Garlic, ground, one teaspoon
- Yeast, one teaspoon

DIRECTIONS

1. In a mixing container, combine the almond flour, dry basil, dried oregano, salt, xanthan powder, and ground garlic.
2. Get another container, where you will combine the melted unsalted butter and the eggs.
3. As per the instructions on your machine's manual, pour the ingredients into the bread pan, and follow how to mix in the yeast.
4. Put the bread pan in the machine, select the basic bread setting, together with the bread size and crust type, if available, then press start once you have closed the machine's lid.
5. When the bread is ready, using oven mitts, remove the bread pan from the machine. Use a stainless spatula to extract the bread from the pan and turn the pan upside down on a metallic rack where the bread will cool off before slicing it.

Nutritions *(Per serving):*

Calories: 140 kcal   *Protein: 5 g*
Carbohydrates: 2.8 g   *Fat: 14 g*

134. HERBS FOCACCIA BREAD

| **PREPARATION:** 20MIN | **COOKING:** 1 H | **SERVES:** 6 |

INGREDIENTS

- Three-quarters of a cup warm water
- 1 tsp. Of dried active yeast
- Rosemary fresh, one teaspoon
- Parsley fresh, one teaspoon
- Thyme fresh, one teaspoon
- Sea salt, one teaspoon
- Common salt, half a teaspoon
- Baking powder, two-thirds of a teaspoon
- Swerve sweetener, one teaspoon
- 1 ½ cups fine almond flour
- 1 tsp. Of extra virgin olive oil

DIRECTIONS

1. In a mixing container, combine the almond flour, baking powder, rosemary fresh, parsley fresh, thyme fresh, sea salt, common salt, and swerve sweetener.
2. Get another mixing container and combine the warm water and extra virgin olive oil.
3. As per the instructions on your machine's manual, pour the ingredients into the bread pan, and follow how to mix in the yeast.
4. Place the bread pan on the machine, select the basic bread setting, together with the bread size and crust type, if available, then press start once you have closed the machine's lid.
5. When the bread is ready, using oven mitts, remove the bread pan from the machine. Use a stainless spatula to extract the bread from the pan and turn the pan upside down on a metallic rack where the bread will cool off before slicing it.

Nutritions *(Per serving):*

Calories: 90 kcal
Carbohydrates: 8 g

Protein: 3 g
Fat: 14 g

135. MOZZARELLA HERBS BREAD

PREPARATION: 5 MIN | **COOKING:** 30 MIN | **SERVES:** 8

INGREDIENTS

- Grated cheese mozzarella, one cup
- Grated cheese parmesan, half a cup
- Salt, half a teaspoon
- Baking powder, one teaspoon
- Almond flour, one cup
- Coconut flour, one cup
- Warm water, half a cup
- Stevia, one teaspoon
- Thyme, dried, a quarter teaspoon
- Garlic, ground, one teaspoon
- Basil, dried, one teaspoon
- Olive oil, extra virgin, one teaspoon
- Unsalted melted butter, two teaspoons
- A third cup unsweetened almond milk

DIRECTIONS

1. In a mixing container, mix the almond flour, baking powder, salt, parmesan cheese, mozzarella cheese, coconut flour, dried basil, dried thyme, garlic powder, and stevia powder.
2. Get another mixing container and mix warm water, unsweetened almond milk, melted unsalted butter, and extra virgin olive oil.
3. As per the instructions on your machine's manual, pour the ingredients in the bread pan and follow how to mix in the yeast.
4. Put the bread pan in the machine, select the basic bread setting, together with the bread size and crust type, if available, then press start once you have closed the machine's lid.
5. When the bread is ready, using oven mitts, remove the bread pan from the machine. Use a stainless spatula to extract the bread from the pan and turn the pan upside down on a metallic rack where the bread will cool off before slicing it.

Nutritions *(Per serving):*

Calories: 120 kcal
Carbohydrates: 5 g

Protein: 4 g
Fat: 4 g

136. ITALIAN HERBS LOAF

PREPARATION: 20MIN | **COOKING:** 1 H | **SERVES:** 6

INGREDIENTS

- Almond flour, one and a half cup full
- Romano cheese grated, a third cup full
- Ground onion, half a teaspoon
- Ground garlic, half a teaspoon
- Dried oregano, half a teaspoon
- Half tsp. Of basil dried
- Baking powder, half a teaspoon
- Salt, two-thirds of a teaspoon
- Olive oil, extra virgin, a quarter cup full
- Swerve sweetener, two teaspoons
- Yeast, one teaspoon
- 1 cup warm water

DIRECTIONS

1. In a mixing container, combine the almond flour, baking powder, dried basil, dry oregano, salt, ground garlic, grated Romano cheese, and ground onion.
2. In a separate mixing container, mix the warm water and extra virgin olive oil.
3. As per the instructions on your machine's manual, pour the ingredients into the bread pan, and follow how to mix in the yeast.
4. Put the bread pan in the machine, select the basic bread setting, together with the bread size and crust type, if available, then press start once you have closed the machine's lid.
5. When the bread is ready, using oven mitts, remove the bread pan from the machine. Use a stainless spatula to extract the bread from the pan and turn the pan upside down on a metallic rack where the bread will cool off before slicing it.

Nutritions *(Per serving):*

Calories: 140 kcal
Carbohydrates: 2.8 g

Protein: 5 g
Fat: 14 g

137. CHILI HERBS BREAD

PREPARATION: 20MIN   **COOKING:** 1 H   **SERVES:** 4

INGREDIENTS

- 1 cup fine almond flour
- Sea salt, one teaspoon
- Yeast, one teaspoon
- Olive oil, extra virgin, two teaspoons
- Basil fresh, two teaspoons
- Thyme, fresh, two teaspoons
- Oregano, fresh, two teaspoons
- 2 tsp. Of crushed garlic cloves
- 1 lime zest
- 2 tsp. Of cayenne pepper powder
- Half a cup warm water

DIRECTIONS

1. Get a mixing container and combine the almond flour, sea salt, freshly chopped basil, freshly chopped thyme, freshly chopped oregano, crushed garlic, and ground cayenne pepper.
2. Get another mixing container and combine the warm water, extra virgin olive oil, and lime zest in it.
3. As per the instructions on your machine's manual, pour the ingredients into the bread pan, and follow how to mix in the yeast.
4. Place the bread pan on the machine, and select the basic bread setting, together with the bread size and crust type if available, then press start once you have closed the lid of the machine.
5. When the bread is ready, using oven mitts, remove the bread pan from the machine. Use a stainless spatula to extract the bread from the pan and turn the pan upside down on a metallic rack where the bread will cool off before slicing it.

Nutritions *(Per serving):*

Calories: 120 kcal   *Protein: 5 g*
Carbohydrates: 5 g   *Fat: 4 g*

138. SAVORY HERB BLEND BREAD

PREPARATION: 20MIN   **COOKING:** 1 H   **SERVES:** 16

INGREDIENTS

- 1 cup almond flour
- 1/2 cup coconut flour
- 1 cup parmesan cheese
- 3/4 tsp baking powder
- 3 eggs
- 3 tbsp coconut oil
- 1/2 tbsp rosemary
- 1/2 tsp thyme, ground
- 1/2 tsp sage, ground
- 1/2 tsp oregano
- 1/2 tsp garlic powder
- 1/2 tsp onion powder
- 1/4 tsp salt

DIRECTIONS

1. Light beat eggs and coconut oil together before adding to bread machine pan.
2. Add all the remaining ingredients to the bread machine pan.
3. Set bread machine to the gluten-free setting.
4. When the bread is baked, remove the bread machine pan from the bread machine.
5. Let cool before transferring to a cooling rack.
6. You can store your bread for up to 7 days.

Nutritions *(Per serving):*

Calories: 170 kcal
Carbohydrates: 6 g

Protein: 9 g
Fat: 15 g

CHAPTER 11
Sweet Bread and Cake

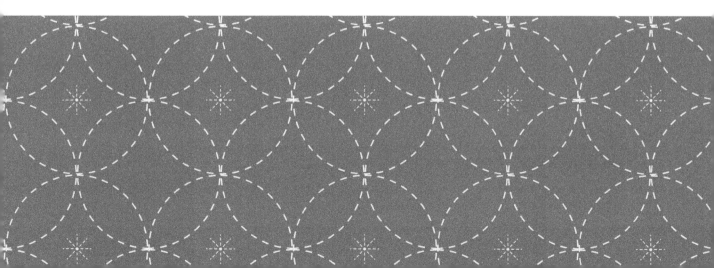

139. CHOCOLATE DATE SESAME BREAD

PREPARATION: 10 MIN | **COOKING:** 3-4 H | **SERVES:** 12

INGREDIENTS

- ½ cup butter softened
- 1½ teaspoons salt
- 3 tablespoons sugar
- ¾ cup milk
- ¾ cup water
- 4 cups flour
- ½ cup chocolate
- 2 tablespoons cocoa powder
- 3 tablespoons sesame seeds
- ½ cup dates pitted
- 1 tablespoon fresh yeast

DIRECTIONS

1. Sift the flour. Cut the dates finely. Rub the chocolate on a fine grater.
2. Combine the cocoa and water, and stir well so that there are no lumps. Add the milk and stir again.
3. Put the softened butter in the bread container. Then add salt, sugar, the mixture of cocoa and milk, chocolate, and sesame. Then put in the flour and yeast.
4. Roll dates in flour
5. Turn on the bread maker.
6. After finishing, take out the bread container and take out the hot bread. Cool it for 1 hour on a grate, covered with a towel.

Nutritions *(Per serving):*

Calories: 315 kcal
Fat: 11.8 g

Carbohydrates: 46.7 g
Protein: 6.5 g

140. SWEET YOGURT CHERRY BREAD

PREPARATION: 5 MIN	**COOKING:** 2 H 30 MIN	**SERVES:** 8

INGREDIENTS

- ½ cup warm water
- ½ cup fruit yogurt
- 2 ½ tablespoons sugar
- 2 cups flour
- 1 ½ teaspoons yeast
- ½ cup dried cherries

DIRECTIONS

1. Combine the ingredients in the bread maker in the manner indicated in your instructions.
2. Enable the program.
3. After it finishes, take out the bread and cool it on a grate.

Nutritions *(Per serving):*

Calories: 198 kcal
Fat: 0.8 g

Carbohydrates: 42.2 g
Protein: 5.5 g

141. CHOCOLATE BREAD

PREPARATION: 10 MIN **COOKING:** 2 H 30 **SERVES:** 8

INGREDIENTS

- 1 cup water
- 2 1/3 cups wholemeal flour
- ½ cup wheat flour
- ½ cup rice flour
- ¾ cup dark chocolate
- ½ cup sour cream
- 1 tablespoon butter
- 1 ½ tablespoons cocoa
- 1 tablespoon sugar
- 1 teaspoon bread machine yeast
- 1 teaspoon salt

DIRECTIONS

1. In the bowl of the bread maker, pour in water and add sour cream.
2. Top with flour. In the corners of the bowl, pour cocoa powder, yeast, sugar, and salt so that they do not come in contact.
3. Turn on the Knead program. When the dough turns into a ball, press pause and add the butter. Continue the kneading dough.
4. Put the dough into a bowl and put it in a warm place for 1 hour.
5. The dough should increase 2-3 times.
6. Transfer the dough to the table, lightly pouring the surface of the table with flour.
7. Cut the chocolate into small pieces. Roll the dough into an oval-shaped formation. Top with the pieces of chocolate.
8. Roll the dough into a roll.
9. Transfer the dough to the bread maker and leave it for 1 hour.
10. Bake bread in bread maker in the Baking mode for 30 minutes.
11. Serve chocolate bread with tea, milk, or coffee. Chocolate bread is suitable for making dessert sandwiches, and perfectly matches condensed milk, nut butter, and confiture.

Nutritions *(Per serving):*

Calories: 183 kcal
Fat: 8.1 g

Carbohydrates: 25.3 g
Protein: 2.6 g

142. RAISIN CAKE

PREPARATION: 10 MIN   **COOKING:** 2 H 30   **SERVES:** 8

INGREDIENTS

- 2 eggs
- ¾ cup butter
- 1/3 cup milk
- 1 teaspoon salt
- 4 tablespoons sugar
- 2 ¾ cups flour
- 2 teaspoons dry yeast
- ¾ cup raisins

DIRECTIONS

1. Scald raisins with boiling water, drain, and dry.
2. Cut butter into slices.
3. In the bread maker's bowl, beat the eggs, pour in the milk, and add the butter.
4. Add salt and sugar.
5. Sift the flour.
6. Put it in a container.
7. Add the dry yeast.
8. Set the bread maker in the desired mode, selecting the cake's weight and the crust's color. Add the raisins after the signal.
9. Remove cake carefully, so as not to burn your hands. Move to a grate and leave until completely cooled. Cover with icing or sprinkle with powdered sugar.
10. Store the cake in a plastic bag in a cool place. On the day of baking, the cake will be airy; the next day, it gets a more dense cake structure.

Nutritions *(Per serving):*

Calories: 396 kcal
Fat: 19.1 g

Carbohydrates: 50.5 g
Sugar: 14.7 g

Protein: 7.1 g

143. DELICIOUS CAKE FOR TEA

PREPARATION: 10 MIN | **COOKING:** 3 H 30 MIN | **SERVES:** 8

INGREDIENTS

- 2 ½ teaspoons yeast
- 3 ½ cups flour
- ½ teaspoon salt
- 6 tablespoons sugar
- 1 bag vanillin
- 6 tablespoons oil
- 3 eggs
- 1 cup water
- 1 cup peeled and diced apples

Note: You can also add nuts or raisins

DIRECTIONS

1. Put all the ingredients in the bread maker in the order given in the instructions.
2. In the process of baking, the bread will rise quite a bit.
3. After cooking, take out the bread and cool it on a grate.

Nutritions *(Per serving):*

Calories: 379 kcal
Fat: 12.5 g
Carbohydrates: 59.1 g

Sugar: 15.1 g
Protein: 8.4 g

144. BRIOCHE

PREPARATION: 10 MIN | **COOKING:** 3 H 30 MIN | **SERVES:** 8

INGREDIENTS

- 1/3 cup warm milk
- 2 tablespoons sugar
- 1 ½ teaspoon active dry yeast
- 2 large eggs
- 2 ½ cups bread flour
- 1 teaspoon salt
- ½ cup butter, melted

DIRECTIONS

1. Put ingredients in the bread maker according to the instructions—first liquid products, then dry, and then dry yeast at the top.
2. When the bread is ready, remove it from the bread maker and cut it into portions.
3. Serve with butter or marmalade jam.

Nutritions *(Per serving):*

Calories: 147 kcal
Fat: 13 g
Carbohydrates: 5.8 g

Protein: 2.6 g

145. LEMON CAKE

PREPARATION: 10 MIN   **COOKING:** 2 H 30 MIN   **SERVES:** 8

INGREDIENTS

- 3 eggs
- ½ cup butter
- ½ teaspoon salt
- 4/5 cup sugar
- 2 ½ cups flour
- 2 ½ teaspoons baking powder
- juice and peel of one small lemon

DIRECTIONS

1. Combine the eggs, sugar, and salt.
2. Beat with a mixer into a thick foam.
3. Wash the lemon carefully. With a small grater, peel the lemon peel and then squeeze the juice.
4. In the bowl of the bread maker, pour in the eggs with sugar foam. Add softened butter, lemon zest, and juice.
5. Mix flour with baking powder.
6. Pour the flour into the bowl of the bread maker.
7. Set to the desired mode, Dough, for 30 minutes, then bake for 2 hours.
8. Turn the cooked cake onto a grate and cool. Sprinkle with powdered sugar.
9. Serve, and enjoy.

Nutritions *(Per serving):*

Calories: 346 kcal
Fat: 13.6 g

Carbohydrates: 51.2 g
Protein: 6.3 g

146. SWEET COCONUT BREAD

PREPARATION: 5 MIN   **COOKING:** 3 H 30 MIN   **SERVES:** 8

INGREDIENTS

- ¾ cup warm milk
- 2 eggs
- 3 cups flour
- 4 tablespoons butter, melted
- 1 teaspoon salt
- 2 tablespoons sugar
- 1 teaspoon rum
- 1 teaspoon dry yeast
- ½ cup dried coconut

DIRECTIONS

1. Put all the ingredients in the bucket, except oil and coconut.
2. Five minutes after the start of the mixing process, add oil.
3. After the signal, add the coconut.
4. Before starting the baking process, you can grease the top with a beaten egg and decorate with coconut shavings. Or, after baking, cover with syrup and powdered sugar.

Nutritions *(Per serving):*

Calories: 367 kcal
Fat: 11.8 g

Carbohydrates: 54.8 g
Protein: 9.5 g

147. PINEAPPLE COCONUT BREAD PINA COLADA

PREPARATION: 5 MIN	**COOKING:** 4 H	**SERVES:** 6

INGREDIENTS

- 2 teaspoons dry yeast
- 2 tablespoons sugar
- 3 ¾ cups flour
- 1 teaspoon salt
- 6 tablespoons coconut shavings
- ½ cup candied, dried pineapple
- 1 ½ tablespoon rum
- 1 tablespoon oil
- 1 cup water

DIRECTIONS

1. Cut pineapple into cubes and douse with boiling water. Do not soak.
2. Place all the ingredients in the bread maker and turn it on to proper mode.
3. You can sprinkle the hot loaf with powdered sugar.
4. Rather than pineapple, you can use any other kind of candied or exotic fruits.

Nutritions *(Per serving):*

Calories: 436 kcal
Fat: 7.1 g

Carbohydrates: 81.6 g
Protein: 8.1 g

148. CHRISTMAS BREAD WITH PEANUT BUTTER

PREPARATION: 10 MIN	**COOKING:** 4 H	**SERVES:** 8

INGREDIENTS

- 1 cup milk
- 3 cups flour
- ½ cup peanut butter
- 1 ½ teaspoons yeast
- 1 tablespoon powdered milk
- zest of lemon or lime
- 1 egg
- 1 tablespoon oil

DIRECTIONS

1. Mix peanut butter with milk and let stand.
2. Crack an egg into the bucket. Pour milk and peanut butter in it, then add the oil.
3. Pour in the flour and then the yeast.
4. The zest can be added at once, but it is possible to add extra ingredients after the signal.
5. Turn the bread maker on the French program.
6. If you like very sweet bread, then you can add sugar.
7. In general, after 4 hours, you will have a very delicious and fragrant bread.

Nutritions *(Per serving):*

Calories: 314 kcal
Fat: 11.5 g

Carbohydrates: 42.5 g
Protein: 11.3 g

149. FRUIT BREAD

PREPARATION: 10 MIN   **COOKING:** 4 H   **SERVES:** 8

INGREDIENTS

- 1 cup orange juice
- ½ cup water
- 2 ½ tablespoons butter
- 2 tablespoons powdered milk
- 2 ½ tablespoons sugar
- 1 teaspoon salt
- 4 cups flour
- 1 ½ teaspoon active dry yeast
- ¾ cup candied fruit (pineapple, coconut, papaya)
- 1 tablespoon flour for packing candied fruits
- ½ cup almond flakes

DIRECTIONS

1. You can add any juice. The most delicious combinations of juice are multifruit, banana-strawberry, pear-apple
2. Put the candied fruit in water, cognac, or juice, then dry it on a paper towel and roll in flour.
3. Almond petals together with candied fruits in a dispenser or a bucket on a signal.
4. Turn on the bread maker program.
5. After the baking is finished, cool the bread on a grate.

Nutritions *(Per serving):*

Calories: 313 kcal
Fat: 4.3 g

Carbohydrates: 60.2 g
Protein: 7.8 g

150. ORANGE BREAD

PREPARATION: 10 MIN | **COOKING:** 4 H | **SERVES:** 8

INGREDIENTS

- 1 ½ teaspoons yeast
- 3 ½ cups flour
- 1 ½ teaspoons salt
- 2 tablespoons sugar
- 2 tablespoons butter
- 1 cup orange juice
- ½ cup milk
- 2 teaspoons orange peel
- ½ teaspoon ground cardamom
- 1 teaspoon turmeric
- dried cranberries to taste

DIRECTIONS

1. Put all the ingredients in the bread maker according to the instructions.
2. Turn on the baking program.
3. After baking, cool the bread on a grate.
4. It is delicious to spread orange marmalade on top and serve with cardamom tea.

Nutritions *(Per serving):*

Calories: 261 kcal
Fat: 3.9 g

Carbohydrates: 49.4 g
Protein: 6.7 g

151. ORANGE POPPY BREAD

PREPARATION: 10 MIN   **COOKING:** 3 H 30 MIN   **SERVES:** 8

INGREDIENTS

- 3 cups flour
- 2/5 cup oat flour
- ¾ cup orange juice
- peels of 2 oranges
- ½ teaspoon salt
- 2 ½ tablespoons sugar
- 2 ½ tablespoons butter
- 1 teaspoon yeast
- 4 tablespoons poppy seeds, fried

DIRECTIONS

1. Put all the ingredients in the bread maker according to the instructions.
2. Turn on the baking program.
3. After baking, cool the bread on a grate.
4. Enjoy!

Nutritions   *(Per serving):*

Calories: 274 kcal   *Protein: 6.7 g*
Fat: 6.4 g
Carbohydrates: 47.5 g

152. BANANA MACADAMIA NUT BREAD

PREPARATION: 10 MIN   **COOKING:** 3 H   **SERVES:** 12

INGREDIENTS

- 2/3 cup warm water
- 3/4 cup mashed bananas
- 2 tablespoons margarine, softened
- 1 egg
- 3 1/4 cups bread flour
- 3 tablespoons white sugar
- 1 1/4 teaspoons salt
- 2 3/4 teaspoons active dry yeast
- 1/2 cup chopped macadamia nuts

DIRECTIONS

1. Combine the ingredients in the bread machine in the order recommended by your manufacturer. Select sweet bread setting and light crust.
2. Add macadamia nuts when indicated by your manufacturer.

Nutritions *(Per serving):*

Calories: 166 kcal   *Carbohydrates: 27.85 g*
Protein: 2.19 g
Fat: 5.36 g

153. BILL'S BRAISIN BREAD

PREPARATION: 10 MIN | **COOKING:** 3 H | **SERVES:** 12

INGREDIENTS

- 1 1/2 cups water
- 1 (.25 ounce) package active dry yeast
- 1 tablespoon white sugar
- 3 cups bread flour
- 1 1/2 cups raisin bran cereal
- 1 teaspoon salt

DIRECTIONS

1. Put the ingredients in the pan of the bread machine in the order recommended by the manufacturer.
2. Select Med Crust cycle; press Start.

Nutritions *(Per serving):*

Calories: 140 kcal
Protein: 4.03 g

Fat: 2.24 g
Carbohydrates: 26.67 g

154. BRANDIED PUMPKIN BREAD

PREPARATION: 20MIN | **COOKING:** 1 H 30 MIN | **SERVES:** 8

INGREDIENTS

- 3 cups bread flour
- 2 1/4 teaspoons bread machine yeast
- 1/4 cup white sugar
- 1/2 teaspoon pumpkin pie spice
- 1 1/4 teaspoons salt
- 2 tablespoons butter, softened
- 3/4 cup canned pumpkin puree
- 1/2 cup water
- 1 1/2 teaspoons brandy

DIRECTIONS

1. Combine flour, yeast, sugar, pumpkin pie spice, salt, butter, pumpkin puree, water, and brandy in the bread machine in the order recommended by the manufacturer.
2. Select the Sweet or Basic/White cycle using the Light crust setting and start the machine. (To make the bread without a bread machine, see Editor's Note.)
3. When the bread is done baking, remove it from the pan and cool on a wire rack.

Note: You may use vanilla extract instead of brandy, and margarine instead of butter, if you prefer.

Nutritions *(Per serving):*

Calories: 153 kcal
Protein: 2.47 g

Fat: 6.33 g
Carbohydrates: 21.97 g

155. BROWN SUGAR BANANA NUT BREAD II

PREPARATION: 5 MIN   **COOKING:** 1 H 30 MIN   **SERVES:** 12

INGREDIENTS

- 1/2 cup milk
- 2 tablespoons butter, softened
- 2 eggs
- 1/4 cup white sugar
- 1/4 cup brown sugar
- 1 1/2 cups all-purpose flour
- 1 teaspoon salt
- 1 teaspoon baking soda
- 1 (.25 ounce) package active dry yeast
- 2 small ripe bananas, sliced
- 1/2 cup chopped walnuts

DIRECTIONS

1. Combine the ingredients in the pan of the bread machine in the order recommended by the manufacturer.
2. Select cycle; press Start. If your machine has a Fruit setting, add the bananas and nuts at the signal, or about 5 minutes before the kneading cycle has finished.

Nutritions *(Per serving):*

Calories: 181 kcal
Protein: 2.98 g
Fat: 8.65 g

Carbohydrates: 23.69 g

156. BROWNIE BREAD

PREPARATION: 10 MIN   **COOKING:** 3 H   **SERVES:** 12

INGREDIENTS

- 1/2 cup unsweetened cocoa powder
- 1/2 cup boiling water
- 2 1/2 teaspoons active dry yeast
- 2 teaspoons white sugar
- 1/2 cup warm water
- 3 cups bread flour
- 2/3 cup white sugar
- 1 teaspoon salt
- 2 tablespoons vegetable oil
- 1 egg yolk

DIRECTIONS

1. In a bowl, melt cocoa powder in boiling water.
2. In a separate bowl, dissolve yeast and two teaspoons of sugar in warm water. Let it stand until creamy, about 10 minutes.
3. Place cocoa mixture, yeast mixture, bread flour, remaining 2/3 cup white sugar, salt, vegetable oil, and egg in bread machine pan. Select basic bread cycle; press Start.

Nutritions *(Per serving):*

Calories: 162 kcal
Protein: 2.51 g

Fat: 5.65 g
Carbohydrates: 22.69 g

157. CHOCOLATE CHIP ALMOND BREAD

PREPARATION: 10 MIN	**COOKING:** 3 H	**SERVES:** 12

INGREDIENTS

- 1 cup warm milk (110 degrees F)
- 1 1/2 teaspoons salt
- 2 tablespoons margarine
- 3 cups bread flour
- 3 tablespoons white sugar
- 2 teaspoons active dry yeast
- 1/2 cup semisweet chocolate chips
- 1/3 cup blanched slivered almonds
- 2 tablespoons unsweetened cocoa powder
- 1 teaspoon almond extract
- 1/2 cup butter
- 1 cup confectioners' sugar
- 2 teaspoons grated orange zest

DIRECTIONS

1. Add the milk, salt, 2 tablespoons of butter or margarine, flour, sugar, and baking powder to your bread maker in the order recommended by the manufacturer. Click Basic or Rapid setting. Press start. When the display shows 0:00, or the second kneading is about to begin, press stop and remove the loaf.
2. Add the chocolate chips, almonds, cacao powder, and almond extract to the batter. Go back to the bread maker and finish the cycle. Serve warm with orange butter.
3. To make Orange Butter: Combine 1/2 cup butter or margarine, 1 cup confectioners' sugar, and the zest of a small orange in a food processor until blended.

Nutritions *(Per serving):*

Calories: 174 kcal
Protein: 2.65 g
Fat: 5.82 g

Carbohydrates: 22.80 g

158. CHOCOLATE CHIP BREAD I

PREPARATION: 10 MIN | **COOKING:** 2 H 50 MIN | **SERVES:** 15

INGREDIENTS

- 1/4 cup water
- 1 cup milk
- 1 egg
- 3 cups bread flour
- 3 tablespoons brown sugar
- 2 tablespoons white sugar
- 1 teaspoon salt
- 1 teaspoon ground cinnamon
- 1 1/2 teaspoons active dry yeast
- 2 tablespoons margarine, softened
- 3/4 cup semisweet chocolate chips

DIRECTIONS

1. Put ingredients in the pan of the bread machine in the order recommended by the manufacturer.
2. Select the 'Mix Bread' cycle or the setting that allows ingredients such as seeds or fruit to be folded into the dough; press Start. Combine the chocolate chips at the signal, or about 5 minutes before the kneading cycle has finished. Take the loaf out of the pan and allow it to cool when the cooking cycle is complete.

Nutritions *(Per serving):*

Calories: 176 kcal
Protein: 2.68 g
Fat: 5.84 g

Carbohydrates: 22.82 g

159. CHOCOLATE CHIP BREAD II

PREPARATION: 5 MIN | **COOKING:** 2 H 10 MIN | **SERVES:** 12

INGREDIENTS

- 1 (.25 ounce) package active dry yeast
- 3 cups bread flour
- 2 tablespoons brown sugar
- 2 tablespoons white sugar
- 1 teaspoon salt
- 1 teaspoon ground cinnamon
- 4 tablespoons butter, softened
- 1 egg
- 1 cup warm milk
- 1/4 cup warm water
- 1 cup semisweet chocolate chips

DIRECTIONS

1. Put the ingredients in the pan of the bread machine in the order recommended by the manufacturer. Select White Bread cycle; press Start.
2. If your machine has a Fruit setting, add chocolate chips at the signal or about 5 minutes before the kneading cycle has finished.

Nutritions *(Per serving):*

Calories: 180 kcal
Protein: 2.72 g
Fat: 5.90 g

Carbohydrates: 21.82 g

160. PANETTONE II

PREPARATION: 5 MIN　　　**COOKING:** 3 H　　　**SERVES:** 10

INGREDIENTS

- 3/4 cup warm water
- 1/4 cup butter
- 2 eggs
- 1 1/2 teaspoons vanilla extract
- 3 1/4 cups bread flour
- 2 tablespoons white sugar
- 2 tablespoons dry milk powder
- 1 1/2 teaspoons salt
- 2 teaspoons bread machine yeast
- 1/2 cup chopped mixed dried fruit

DIRECTIONS

1. Put all of the ingredients except for the mixed fruit into the pan of your bread machine in the order directed by the manufacturer.
2. Select Sweet or Basic/White bread cycle, and use the Medium or Light crust color. Do not use the delay cycles. Add the fruit 5 to 10 minutes before the last kneading cycle ends or when the raisin or nut signal starts.

Nutritions *(Per serving):*

Calories: 138 kcal　　　*Carbohydrates: 25.5 g*
Protein: 4.49 g
Fat: 1.79 g

161. BROWN AND WHITE SUGAR BREAD

PREPARATION: 5 MIN　　　**COOKING:** 2 H 55 MIN　　　**SERVES:** 12

INGREDIENTS

- 1 cup milk (room temperature)
- ¼ cup butter softened
- 1 egg
- ¼ cup light brown sugar
- ¼ cup granulated white sugar
- 2 tablespoons ground cinnamon
- ¼ teaspoon salt
- 3 cups bread flour
- 2 teaspoons bread machine yeast

DIRECTIONS

1. Place all ingredients in the baking pan of the bread machine in the order recommended by the manufacturer.
2. Place the baking pan in the bread machine and close the lid.
3. Select Sweet Bread setting and then Medium Crust.
4. Press the start button.
5. Carefully remove the baking pan from the machine and then invert the bread loaf onto a wire rack to cool completely before slicing.
6. With a sharp knife, cut bread loaf into desired-sized slices and serve.

Nutritions *(Per serving):*

Calories: 195 kcal　　　*Fiber: 1.6 g*
Fat: 5 g　　　*Sugar: 8.2 g*
Carbohydrates: 33.2 g　　　*Protein: 4.7 g*

162. MOLASSES BREAD

PREPARATION: 5 MIN | **COOKING:** 4 H | **SERVES:** 12

INGREDIENTS

- 1/3 cup milk
- ¼ cup water
- 3 tablespoons molasses
- 3 tablespoons butter, softened
- 2 cups bread flour
- 1¾ cups whole-wheat flour
- 2 tablespoons white sugar
- 1 teaspoon salt
- 2¼ teaspoons quick-rising yeast

DIRECTIONS

1. Place all ingredients in the baking pan of the bread machine in the order recommended by the manufacturer.
2. Place the baking pan in the bread machine and close the lid.
3. Select Light Browning setting.
4. Press the start button.
5. Carefully remove the baking pan from the machine and then invert the bread loaf onto a wire rack to cool completely before slicing.
6. With a sharp knife, cut bread loaf into desired-sized slices and serve.

Nutritions *(Per serving):*

Calories: 205 kcal
Fat: 3.9 g
Carbohydrates: 37.4 g

Fiber: 3.1 g
Sugar: 5.1 g
Protein: 5.6 g

163. HONEY BREAD

PREPARATION: 5 MIN | **COOKING:** 2 H | **SERVES:** 16

INGREDIENTS

- 1 cup plus 1 tablespoon milk
- 3 tablespoons honey
- 3 tablespoons butter, melted
- 3 cups bread flour
- 1½ teaspoons salt
- 2 teaspoons active dry yeast

DIRECTIONS

1. Place all ingredients in the baking pan of the bread machine in the order recommended by the manufacturer.
2. Place the baking pan in the bread machine and close the lid.
3. Select White Bread setting and then Medium Crust.
4. Press the start button.
5. Carefully remove the baking pan from the machine and then invert the bread loaf onto a wire rack to cool completely before slicing.
6. With a sharp knife, cut bread loaf into desired-sized slices and serve.

Nutritions *(Per serving):*

Calories: 126 kcal
Fat: 2.7 g

Carbohydrates: 22.1 g
Sugar: 4 g

Protein: 3.2 g

164. MAPLE SYRUP BREAD

PREPARATION: 5 MIN   **COOKING:** 3 H   **SERVES:** 12

INGREDIENTS

- 1 cup buttermilk
- 2 tablespoons maple syrup
- 2 tablespoons vegetable oil
- 2 tablespoons non-fat dry milk powder
- 1 cup whole-wheat flour
- 2 cups bread flour
- 1 teaspoon salt
- 1½ teaspoons bread machine yeast

DIRECTIONS

1. Place all ingredients in the baking pan of the bread machine in the order recommended by the manufacturer.
2. Place the baking pan in the bread machine and close the lid.
3. Select the Basic setting.
4. Press the start button.
5. Carefully remove the baking pan from the machine and then invert the bread loaf onto a wire rack to cool completely before slicing.
6. With a sharp knife, cut bread loaf into desired-sized slices and serve.

Nutritions *(Per serving):*

Calories: 151 kcal
Fat: 2.6 g

Carbohydrates: 26.1 g
Protein: 4.7 g

165. PEANUT BUTTER AND JELLY BREAD

PREPARATION: 5 MIN | **COOKING:** 3 H | **SERVES:** 12

INGREDIENTS

- 1 cup water
- 1½ tablespoons vegetable oil
- ½ cup peanut butter
- ½ cup blackberry jelly
- 1 tablespoon white sugar
- 1 teaspoon salt
- 1 cup whole-wheat flour
- 2 cups bread flour
- 1½ teaspoons active dry yeast

DIRECTIONS

1. Place all ingredients in the baking pan of the bread machine in the order recommended by the manufacturer.
2. Place the baking pan in the bread machine and close the lid.
3. Select Sweet Bread setting.
4. Press the start button.
5. Carefully remove the baking pan from the machine and then invert the bread loaf onto a wire rack to cool completely before slicing.
6. With a sharp knife, cut bread loaf into desired-sized slices and serve.

Nutritions *(Per serving):*

Calories: 218 kcal
Fat: 7.2 g

Carbohydrates: 31.6 g
Protein: 6.7 g

166. RAISIN BREAD

PREPARATION: 5 MIN | **COOKING:** 3 H | **SERVES:** 12

INGREDIENTS

- 1 cup water
- 2 tablespoons margarine
- 3 cups bread flour
- 3 tablespoons white sugar
- 1 teaspoon salt
- 1 teaspoon ground cinnamon
- 2½ teaspoons active dry yeast
- ¾ cup golden raisins

DIRECTIONS

1. Place all ingredients (except for raisins) in the bread machine's baking pan in the order recommended by the manufacturer.
2. Place the baking pan in the bread machine and close the lid.
3. Select Sweet Bread setting.
4. Press the start button.
5. Wait for the bread machine to beep before adding the raisins.
6. Carefully remove the baking pan from the machine and then invert the bread loaf onto a wire rack to cool completely before slicing.
7. With a sharp knife, cut bread loaf into desired-sized slices and serve.

Nutritions *(Per serving):*

Calories: 172 kcal
Fat: 2.3 g

Carbohydrates: 34.5 g
Protein: 3.9 g

167. CURRANT BREAD

PREPARATION: 10 MIN   **COOKING:** 3 H 30 MIN   **SERVES:** 10

INGREDIENTS

- 1¼ cups warm milk
- 2 tablespoons light olive oil
- 2 tablespoons maple syrup
- 3 cups bread flour
- 2 teaspoons ground cardamom
- 1 teaspoon salt
- 2 teaspoons active dry yeast
- ½ cup currants
- ½ cup cashews, chopped finely

DIRECTIONS

1. Place all ingredients (except for currants and cashews) in the bread machine's baking pan in the order recommended by the manufacturer.
2. Place the baking pan in the bread machine and close the lid.
3. Select the Basic setting.
4. Press the start button.
5. Wait for the bread machine to beep before adding the currants and cashews.
6. Carefully remove the baking pan from the machine and then invert the bread loaf onto a wire rack to cool completely before slicing.
7. With a sharp knife, cut bread loaf into desired-sized slices and serve.

Nutritions *(Per serving):*

Calories: 232 kcal
Fat: 7.1 g

Carbohydrates: 36.4 g
Protein: 6.4 g

168. PINEAPPLE JUICE BREAD

PREPARATION: 5 MIN	**COOKING:** 3 H	**SERVES:** 12

INGREDIENTS

- ¾ cup fresh pineapple juice
- 1 egg
- 2 tablespoons vegetable oil
- 2½ tablespoons honey
- ¾ teaspoon salt
- 3 cups bread flour
- 2 tablespoons dry milk powder
- 2 teaspoons quick-rising yeast

DIRECTIONS

1. Place all ingredients in the baking pan of the bread machine in the order recommended by the manufacturer.
2. Place the baking pan in the bread machine and close the lid.
3. Select Sweet Bread setting and then Light Crust.
4. Press the start button.
5. Carefully remove the baking pan from the machine and then invert the bread loaf onto a wire rack to cool completely before slicing.
6. With a sharp knife, cut bread loaf into desired-sized slices and serve.

Nutritions *(Per serving):*

Calories: 168 kcal
Fat: 3 g

Carbohydrates: 30.5 g
Protein: 4.5 g

169. MOCHA BREAD

PREPARATION: 5 MIN | **COOKING:** 2 H | **SERVES:** 12

INGREDIENTS

- 1/8 cup coffee-flavored liqueur
- ¼ cup water
- 1 (5-ounce) can evaporated milk
- 1 teaspoon salt
- 1½ teaspoons vegetable oil
- 3 cups bread flour
- 2 tablespoons brown sugar
- 1 teaspoon active dry yeast
- ¼ cup semi-sweet mini chocolate chips

DIRECTIONS

1. Put the ingredients (except the chocolate chips) in the bread machine's baking pan in the order recommended by the manufacturer.
2. Place the baking pan in the bread machine and close the lid.
3. Select the Dough cycle.
4. Press the start button.
5. After the Dough cycle completes, remove the dough from the bread pan and place it onto a lightly floured surface.
6. With a plastic wrap, cover the dough for about 10 minutes.
7. Uncover the dough and roll it into a rectangle.
8. Sprinkle the dough with chocolate chips and then shape it into a loaf.
9. Now, place the dough into a greased loaf pan.
10. With a plastic wrap, cover the loaf pan and set it in a warm place for 45 minutes or until doubled in size.
11. Preheat your oven to 375°F.
12. Bake for approximately 24 – 30 minutes or until a wooden skewer inserted in the center comes out clean.
13. Remove the loaf pan from the oven and place onto a wire rack to cool for about 10 minutes.
14. Now, invert bread onto the wire rack to cool completely before slicing.
15. Using a sharp knife, cut the bread loaf into desired-sized slices and serve.

Nutritions *(Per serving):*

Calories: 179 kcal
Fat: 4.6 g

Carbohydrates: 29.8 g
Protein: 4.2 g

CHAPTER 12
Pizza And Focaccia

170. HUBBY'S PIZZA BREAD

PREPARATION: 10 MIN   **COOKING:** 2-4 H   **SERVES:** 14

INGREDIENTS

- 1 1/4 cups milk
- 1 1/2 tablespoons butter, softened
- 3/4 cup shredded Cheddar cheese
- 16 ounces sliced pepperoni sausage
- 1 1/2 tablespoons white sugar
- 1 teaspoon salt
- 1 tablespoon grated Parmesan cheese
- 1 (.25 ounce) package active dry yeast
- 3 1/2 cups bread flour

DIRECTIONS

1. Into the pan of your bread machine, put the ingredients according to the order suggested by the manufacturer.
2. Set the machine to the Bread/Light Crust cycle and then push the Start button.

Nutritions *(Per serving):*

Calories: 314 kcal   Protein: 13 g
Carbohydrates: 25.6 g   Fat: 17.2 g

171. PEPPERONI PIZZA BREAD

PREPARATION: 10 MIN   **COOKING:** 2-4 H   **SERVES:** 12

INGREDIENTS

- 1 3/8 cups water
- 3 cups bread flour
- 2 tablespoons dry milk powder
- 2 tablespoons white sugar
- 1 1/2 teaspoons salt
- 2 tablespoons butter
- 1/2 cup pepperoni sausage, chopped
- 1/3 cup shredded mozzarella cheese
- 1 tablespoon grated Parmesan cheese
- 1/3 cup canned mushrooms
- 1/4 cup dried minced onion
- 3/4 teaspoon garlic powder
- 2 1/2 teaspoons active dry yeast

DIRECTIONS

1. In order recommended by the manufacturer, put ingredients in bread machine pan. Choose a basic bread setting and start.
2. Baking bread in the oven: Choose manual/dough cycle. Form dough, when the cycle is completed, put in a greased loaf pan. Let rise till doubled in size in a warm area. In preheated 175°C/350°F oven, bake for 35-45 minutes or till inserted thermometer in the middle of load reads 95°C/200°F.

Nutritions *(Per serving):*

Calories: 94 kcal
Protein: 4.1 g

Fat: 6.8 g
Carbohydrates: 4.5 g

172. BREAD MACHINE FOCACCIA

PREPARATION: 10 MIN	**COOKING:** 2-4 H	**SERVES:** 12

INGREDIENTS

- 1 cup lukewarm water
- 2 tablespoons olive oil
- 1/2 teaspoon salt
- 2 teaspoons chopped garlic
- 1 tablespoon chopped fresh rosemary
- 3 cups bread flour
- 1 1/2 teaspoons active dry yeast
- 2 tablespoons olive oil
- 1 1/2 teaspoons chopped fresh rosemary

DIRECTIONS

1. Put the water, 2 tablespoons of olive oil, salt, garlic, 1 tablespoon of rosemary, bread flour, and yeast into the bread machine pan following the manufacturer's suggested order of ingredients. Choose the Dough cycle on the machine and press the Start button.
2. Take the dough out from the machine once the whole cycle is done. Flatten the dough out in a 13x9-inch baking pan or a 12-inch pizza pan. Poke the dough with your fingers about an inch apart. Use a brush to coat the dough with the remaining olive oil; top it off with the remaining rosemary.
3. Preheat the oven to 400°F (200°C). Use a plastic wrap to cover the focaccia while the oven is preheating.
4. Put in the preheated oven and bake for 20-25 minutes until it turns golden brown. Allow it to cool down for 5 minutes before serving.

Nutritions *(Per serving):*

Calories: 166 kcal
Fat: 5.1 g

Carbohydrates: 25.2 g
Protein: 4.3 g

173. PARMESAN FOCACCIA BREAD

PREPARATION: 10 MIN   **COOKING:** 2-4 H   **SERVES:** 17

INGREDIENTS

- 1 1/3 cups warm water
- 1 teaspoon white sugar
- 1 teaspoon salt
- 4 1/4 cups bread flour
- 1 teaspoon lecithin
- 3 teaspoons bread machine yeast
- 4 teaspoons olive oil
- 4 teaspoons dried oregano
- 1/3 cup olive oil
- 1/3 cup grated Parmesan cheese

DIRECTIONS

1. Follow the order of putting the ingredients into the bread machine recommended by the manufacturer. Choose the Dough setting on the machine and press the Start button.
2. Once the dough has risen in size once in the bread machine, place it in a greased 8-inch round baking tin. Let it rise until the size doubles.
3. With your fingers, create holes all over the dough up to the bottom of the baking tin. Let it sit for 5 or 10 more minutes.
4. Drizzle the olive oil evenly on top of the dough and top it off with parmesan cheese.
5. Place the baking tin in the middle part of the preheated 400°F (205°C) oven and let it bake for about 20 minutes until it turns golden brown.

Nutritions *(Per serving):*

Calories: 104 kcal
Carbohydrates: 14.5 g

Protein: 2.8 g
Fat: 3.8 g

174. SUN-DRIED TOMATO FOCACCIA

PREPARATION: 10 MIN | **COOKING:** 2-4 H | **SERVES:** 12

INGREDIENTS

- 1 cup water
- 3 cups bread flour
- 2 tablespoons dry milk powder
- 3 1/2 tablespoons white sugar
- 1 teaspoon salt
- 3 tablespoons margarine
- 2 teaspoons active dry yeast
- 1/2 cup chopped sun-dried tomatoes
- 2 tablespoons olive oil
- 2 tablespoons Parmesan cheese
- 2 teaspoons dried rosemary, crushed
- 1 teaspoon garlic salt
- 1 cup shredded mozzarella cheese

DIRECTIONS

1. In the bread machine, put in the water, flour, powdered milk, sugar, salt, butter or margarine, tomatoes, and yeast following the order of ingredients recommended by the manufacturer. Choose the Dough cycle on the machine and press the Start button. The dough will weigh 1/2 pound.
2. Once the machine has finished the whole cycle, remove the dough from the bread machine. Use your hands to knead the dough for 1 minute. Put it on a greased bowl and flip the dough a couple of times to grease the dough's outside surface. Use a damp cloth to coat the batter and allow it to rise in volume in a warm place for 15 minutes.
3. Sprinkle the cornmeal on the bottom of a 15x10-inch baking tray. Roll the dough out so that it fits into the baking tray. Use your fingertips to create dents on the dough. Use a brush to coat the top of the dough with oil and use a slightly wet cloth to cover it. Let it rise in volume for 30 minutes.
4. Top it off with garlic salt, parmesan, mozzarella, and rosemary.
5. Put it in the preheated 400°F (205°C) oven and bake for 15 minutes until it turns brown. Let it cool down a bit and slice it into square shapes before serving.

Nutritions *(Per serving):*

Calories: 205 kcal
Protein: 6.9 g

Fat: 14.7 g
Carbohydrates: 12.5 g

CHAPTER 13
Gluten-Free Bread

175. GLUTEN-FREE SIMPLE SANDWICH BREAD

PREPARATION: 5 MIN | **COOKING:** 1 H | **SERVES:** 12

INGREDIENTS

- 1 1/2 cups sorghum flour
- 1 cup tapioca starch or potato starch (not potato flour!)
- 1/2 cup gluten-free millet flour or gluten-free oat flour
- 2 teaspoons xanthan gum
- 1 1/4 teaspoons fine sea salt
- 2 1/2 teaspoons gluten-free yeast for bread machines
- 1 1/4 cups warm water
- 3 tablespoons extra virgin olive oil
- 1 tablespoon honey or raw agave nectar
- 1/2 teaspoon mild rice vinegar or lemon juice
- 2 organic free-range eggs, beaten

DIRECTIONS

1. Combine dry ingredients except for yeast, and reserve.
2. Add the liquid ingredients to the bread maker pan first, then gently pour the mixed dry ingredients on top of the liquid.
3. Make a well in the middle of the dry ingredients and add the yeast.
4. Set for Rapid 1 hour 20 minutes, medium crust color, and press Start.
5. Place on a chilling rack for 15 minutes before slicing to serve.

Nutritions *(Per serving):*

Calories: 137 kcal
Fat: 4.6 g

Carbohydrates: 22.1 g
Protein: 2.4 g

176. GRAIN-FREE CHIA BREAD

PREPARATION: 5 MIN	**COOKING:** 3 H	**SERVES:** 12

INGREDIENTS

- 1 cup warm water
- 3 large organic eggs, room temperature
- 1/4 cup olive oil
- 1 tablespoon apple cider vinegar
- 1 cup gluten-free chia seeds, ground to flour
- 1 cup almond meal flour
- 1/2 cup potato starch
- 1/4 cup coconut flour
- 3/4 cup millet flour
- 1 tablespoon xanthan gum
- 1 1/2 teaspoons salt
- 2 tablespoons sugar
- 3 tablespoons nonfat dry milk
- 6 teaspoons instant yeast

DIRECTIONS

1. Whisk wet ingredients and add to the bread maker pan.
2. Whisk dry ingredients, except yeast, together and add on top of wet ingredients.
3. Make a well in the dry ingredients and add yeast.
4. Select Whole Wheat cycle, light crust color, and press Start.
5. Allow to cool completely before serving.

Nutritions *(Per serving):*

Calories: 375 kcal
Fat: 18.3 g

Carbohydrates: 42 g
Protein: 12.2 g

177. GLUTEN-FREE BROWN BREAD

PREPARATION: 5 MIN | **COOKING:** 3 H | **SERVES:** 12

INGREDIENTS

- 2 large eggs, lightly beaten
- 1 3/4 cups warm water
- 3 tablespoons canola oil
- 1 cup brown rice flour
- 3/4 cup oat flour
- 1/4 cup tapioca starch
- 1 1/4 cups potato starch
- 1 1/2 teaspoons salt
- 2 tablespoons brown sugar
- 2 tablespoons gluten-free flaxseed meal
- 1/2 cup nonfat dry milk powder
- 2 1/2 teaspoons xanthan gum
- 3 tablespoons psyllium, whole husks
- 2 1/2 teaspoons gluten-free yeast for bread machines

DIRECTIONS

1. Add the eggs, water, and canola oil to the bread maker pan and stir until combined.
2. Whisk all of the dry ingredients except the yeast together in a large mixing bowl.
3. Add the dry ingredients above the wet ingredients.
4. Make a well in the middle of the dry ingredients and add the yeast.
5. Set the Gluten-Free cycle, medium crust color, and press Start.
6. When the bread is done, lay the pan on its side to cool before slicing to serve.

Nutritions *(Per serving):*

Calories: 201 kcal
Fat: 5.7 g

Carbohydrates: 35.5 g
Protein: 5.1 g

178. EASY GLUTEN-FREE, DAIRY-FREE BREAD

PREPARATION: 15 MIN | **COOKING:** 2 H | **SERVES:** 12

INGREDIENTS

- 1 1/2 cups warm water
- 2 teaspoons active dry yeast
- 2 teaspoons sugar
- 2 eggs, room temperature
- 1 egg white, room temperature
- 1 1/2 tablespoons apple cider vinegar
- 4 1/2 tablespoons olive oil
- 3 1/3 cups multi-purpose gluten-free flour

DIRECTIONS

1. Mix the yeast and sugar to the warm water and stir to mix in a large mixing bowl; set aside until foamy, about 8 to 10 minutes.
2. Whisk the two eggs and one egg white together in a separate mixing bowl and add to the bread maker's baking pan.
3. Add apple cider vinegar and oil to the baking pan.
4. Add foamy yeast/water mixture to baking pan.
5. Add the multi-purpose gluten-free flour on top.
6. Set for Gluten-Free bread setting and Start.
7. Remove and invert the pan onto a cooling rack to remove the bread from the baking pan. Chill thoroughly before slicing to serve.

Nutritions *(Per serving):*

Calories: 241 kcal
Fat: 6.8 g

Carbohydrates: 41 g
Protein: 4.5 g

179. GLUTEN-FREE SOURDOUGH BREAD

PREPARATION: 5 MIN | **COOKING:** 3 H | **SERVES:** 12

INGREDIENTS

- 1 cup water
- 3 eggs
- 3/4 cup ricotta cheese
- 1/4 cup honey
- 1/4 cup vegetable oil
- 1 teaspoon cider vinegar
- 3/4 cup gluten-free sourdough starter
- 2 cups white rice flour
- 2/3 cup potato starch
- 1/3 cup tapioca flour
- 1/2 cup dry milk powder
- 3 1/2 teaspoons xanthan gum
- 1 1/2 teaspoons salt

DIRECTIONS

1. Combine wet ingredients and pour into bread maker pan.
2. Mix the dry ingredients in a large mixing bowl, and add on top of the wet ingredients.
3. Select the Gluten-Free cycle and press Start.
4. Remove the pan from the machine and allow the bread to remain in the pan for approximately 10 minutes.
5. Transfer to a cooling rack before slicing.

Nutritions *(Per serving):*

Calories: 299 kcal
Fat: 7.3 g

Carbohydrates: 46 g
Protein: 5.2 g

180. GLUTEN-FREE POTATO BREAD

PREPARATION: 5 MIN | **COOKING:** 3 H | **SERVES:** 12

INGREDIENTS

- 1 medium russet potato, baked, or mashed leftovers
- 2 packets gluten-free quick yeast
- 3 tablespoons honey
- 3/4 cup warm almond milk
- 2 eggs, 1 egg white
- 3 2/3 cups almond flour
- 3/4 cup tapioca flour
- 1 teaspoon sea salt
- 1 teaspoon dried chives
- 1 tablespoon apple cider vinegar
- 1/4 cup olive oil

DIRECTIONS

1. Stir together dry ingredients, except yeast, in a large mixing bowl; set aside.
2. Whisk together the milk, eggs, oil, apple cider, and honey in a separate mixing bowl.
3. Pour the wet ingredients into the bread maker.
4. Add the dry ingredients above the wet ingredients.
5. Create a well in the middle of dry ingredients and add the yeast.
6. Set to Gluten-Free bread setting, light crust color, and press Start.
7. Allow to cool completely before slicing.

Nutritions *(Per serving):*

Calories: 232 kcal
Fat: 13.2 g

Carbohydrates: 17.4 g
Protein: 10.4 g

181. SORGHUM BREAD RECIPE

PREPARATION: 5 MIN   **COOKING:** 3 H   **SERVES:** 12

INGREDIENTS

- 1 1/2 cups sorghum flour
- 1 cup tapioca starch
- 1/2 cup brown or white sweet rice flour
- 1 teaspoon xanthan gum
- 1 teaspoon guar gum
- 1/2 teaspoon salt
- 3 tablespoons sugar
- 2 1/4 teaspoons instant yeast
- 3 eggs (room temperature, lightly beaten)
- 1/4 cup oil
- 1 1/2 teaspoons vinegar
- 1 3/4 cup milk (105 - 115°F)

DIRECTIONS

1. Combine dry ingredients in a bowl, except for the yeast.
2. Add the wet ingredients to the bread maker pan, then add the dry ingredients on top.
3. Make a well in the middle of the dry ingredients and add the yeast.
4. Set to Basic bread cycle, light crust color, and press Start.
5. Remove and lay on its side to cool on a wire rack before serving.

Nutritions *(Per serving):*

Calories: 169 kcal
Fat: 6.3 g

Carbohydrates: 25.8 g
Protein: 3.3 g

182. GLUTEN-FREE CRUSTY BOULE BREAD

PREPARATION: 15 MIN   **COOKING:** 3 H   **SERVES:** 12

INGREDIENTS

- 3 1/4 cups gluten-free flour mix
- 1 tablespoon active dry yeast
- 1 1/2 teaspoons kosher salt
- 1 tablespoon guar gum
- 1 1/3 cups warm water
- 2 large eggs, room temperature
- 2 tablespoons, plus 2 teaspoons olive oil
- 1 tablespoon honey

DIRECTIONS

1. Stir together dry ingredients, except yeast, in a large mixing bowl; set aside.
2. Whisk the water, eggs, oil, and honey in a separate mixing bowl.
3. Pour the wet ingredients into the bread maker.
4. Add the dry ingredients above the wet ingredients.
5. Make a well in the middle of the dry ingredients and add the yeast.
6. Set to Gluten-Free setting and press Start.
7. Remove baked bread and allow to cool completely. Hollow out and fill with soup or dip to use as a boule or slice for serving.

Nutritions *(Per serving):*

Calories: 480 kcal
Fat: 3.2 g

Carbohydrates: 103.9 g
Protein: 2.4 g

183. PALEO BREAD

PREPARATION: 10 MIN | **COOKING:** 3 H | **SERVES:** 16

INGREDIENTS

- 4 tablespoons chia seeds
- 1 tablespoon flax meal
- 3/4 cup, plus 1 tablespoon water
- 1/4 cup coconut oil
- 3 eggs, room temperature
- 1/2 cup almond milk
- 1 tablespoon honey
- 2 cups almond flour
- 1 1/4 cups tapioca flour
- 1/3 cup coconut flour
- 1 teaspoon salt
- 1/4 cup flax meal
- 2 teaspoons cream of tartar
- 1 teaspoon baking soda
- 2 teaspoons active dry yeast

DIRECTIONS

1. Mix the chia seeds and tablespoon of flax meal in a mixing bowl; stir in the water and set aside.
2. Melt the coconut oil in a microwave-safe dish, and let it cool down to lukewarm.
3. Whisk in the eggs, almond milk, and honey.
4. Whisk in the chia seeds and flax meal gel and pour it into the bread maker pan.
5. Whisk the almond flour, tapioca flour, coconut flour, salt, and 1/4 cup flax meal.
6. Whisk cream of tartar and baking soda in a separate bowl and combine it with the other dry ingredients.
7. Place the dry ingredients into the bread machine.
8. Make a little well on top and add the yeast.
9. Start the machine on the Wheat cycle, light or medium crust color, and press Start.
10. Remove to cool completely before slicing to serve.

Nutritions *(Per serving):*

Calories: 190 kcal
Fat: 10.3 g

Carbohydrates: 20.4 g
Protein: 4.5 g

184. GLUTEN-FREE OAT AND HONEY BREAD

PREPARATION: 5 MIN   **COOKING:** 3 H   **SERVES:** 12

INGREDIENTS

- 1 1/4 cups warm water
- 3 tablespoons honey
- 2 eggs
- 3 tablespoons butter, melted
- 1 1/4 cups gluten-free oats
- 1 1/4 cups brown rice flour
- 1/2 cup potato starch
- 2 teaspoons xanthan gum
- 1 1/2 teaspoons sugar
- 3/4 teaspoon salt
- 1 1/2 tablespoons active dry yeast

DIRECTIONS

1. Add ingredients in the order listed above, except for the yeast.
2. Make a well in the middle of the dry ingredients and add the yeast.
3. Select the Gluten-Free cycle, light crust color, and press Start.
4. Remove bread and allow the bread to cool on its side on a cooling rack for 20 minutes before slicing to serve.

Nutritions *(Per serving):*

Calories: 151 kcal
Fat: 4.5 g

Carbohydrates: 27.2 g
Protein: 3.5 g

185. GLUTEN-FREE CINNAMON RAISIN BREAD

PREPARATION: 5 MIN   **COOKING:** 3 H   **SERVES:** 12

INGREDIENTS

- 3/4 cup almond milk
- 2 tablespoons flax meal
- 6 tablespoons warm water
- 1 1/2 teaspoons apple cider vinegar
- 2 tablespoons butter
- 1 1/2 tablespoons honey
- 1 2/3 cups brown rice flour
- 1/4 cup corn starch
- 2 tablespoons potato starch
- 1 1/2 teaspoons xanthan gum
- 1 tablespoon cinnamon
- 1/2 teaspoon salt
- 1 teaspoon active dry yeast
- 1/2 cup raisins

DIRECTIONS

1. Combine flax and water. Let stand for 5 minutes.
2. Whisk dry ingredients in a separate bowl, except for the yeast.
3. Add wet ingredients to the bread machine.
4. Add the dry mixture on top and make a well in the middle of the dry mixture.
5. Add the yeast to the well.
6. Set to Gluten-Free, light crust color, and press Start.
7. After the first kneading and rise cycle, add raisins.
8. Remove to a cooling rack when baked and let cool for 15 minutes before slicing.

Nutritions *(Per serving):*

Calories: 192 kcal
Fat: 4.7 g

Carbohydrates: 38.2 g
Protein: 2.7 g

186. GLUTEN-FREE PUMPKIN PIE BREAD

PREPARATION: 5 MIN   **COOKING:** 2 H 50 MIN   **SERVES:** 12

INGREDIENTS

- 1/4 cup olive oil
- 2 large eggs, beaten
- 1 tablespoon bourbon vanilla extract
- 1 cup canned pumpkin
- 4 tablespoons honey
- 1/4 teaspoon lemon juice
- 1/2 cup buckwheat flour
- 1/4 cup millet flour
- 1/4 cup sorghum flour
- 1/2 cup tapioca starch
- 1 cup light brown sugar
- 2 teaspoons baking powder
- 1 teaspoon baking soda
- 1/2 teaspoon sea salt
- 1 teaspoon xanthan gum
- 1 teaspoon ground cinnamon
- 1 teaspoon allspice
- 1-2 tablespoons peach juice

DIRECTIONS

1. Mix dry ingredients in a bowl and put aside.
2. Add wet ingredients to the pan, except peach juice.
3. Add mixed dry ingredients to the bread maker pan.
4. Set to Sweet bread cycle, light or medium crust color, and press Start.
5. As it begins to mix the ingredients, use a soft silicone spatula to scrape down the sides.
6. If the batter is stiff, add one tablespoon of peach juice at a time until the batter becomes slightly thinner than the muffin batter.
7. Close the lid and allow to bake. Place in a cooling rack for 20 minutes before slicing.

Nutritions *(Per serving):*

Calories: 180 kcal
Fat: 5.5 g

Carbohydrates: 33.1 g
Protein: 2.4 g

187. GLUTEN-FREE PIZZA CRUST

PREPARATION: 10 MIN | **COOKING:** 2 H | **SERVES:** 8

INGREDIENTS

- 3 large eggs, room temperature
- 1/2 cup olive oil
- 1 cup milk
- 1/2 cup water
- 2 cups rice flour
- 1 cup cornstarch, and extra for dusting
- 1/2 cup potato starch
- 1/2 cup sugar
- 2 tablespoons yeast
- 3 teaspoons xanthan gum
- 1 teaspoon salt

DIRECTIONS

1. Beat wet ingredients in another bowl and pour into loaf pan.
2. Combine the dry ingredients except for the yeast and add to the pan.
3. Make a well in the middle of the dry ingredients and add the yeast.
4. Select the Dough cycle and press Start.
5. When the dough is finished, press it out on a surface lightly sprinkled with corn starch and create a pizza shape. Use this dough with your favorite toppings and pizza recipe!

Nutritions *(Per serving):*

Calories: 463 kcal
Fat: 15.8 g

Carbohydrates: 79.2 g
Protein: 7.4 g

188. GLUTEN-FREE WHOLE GRAIN BREAD

PREPARATION: 15 MIN   **COOKING:** 3 H 40 MIN   **SERVES:** 12

INGREDIENTS

- 2/3 cup sorghum flour
- 1/2 cup buckwheat flour
- 1/2 cup millet flour
- 3/4 cup potato starch
- 2 1/4 teaspoons xanthan gum
- 1 1/4 teaspoons salt
- 3/4 cup skim milk
- 1/2 cup water
- 1 tablespoon instant yeast
- 5 teaspoons agave nectar, separated
- 1 large egg, lightly beaten
- 4 tablespoons extra virgin olive oil
- 1/2 teaspoon cider vinegar
- 1 tablespoon poppy seeds

DIRECTIONS

1. Whisk sorghum, buckwheat, millet, potato starch, xanthan gum, and sea salt in a bowl and set aside.
2. Combine milk and water in a glass measuring cup. Heat to between 110°F and 120°F; add 2 teaspoons of agave nectar and yeast and stir to combine. Cover and set aside for a few minutes.
3. Combine the egg, olive oil, remaining agave, and vinegar in another mixing bowl; add yeast and milk mixture. Pour wet ingredients into the bottom of your bread maker.
4. Top with dry ingredients.
5. Select the Gluten-Free cycle, light color crust, and press Start.
6. After the second kneading cycle, sprinkle poppy seeds.
7. Remove pan from the bread machine. Leave the loaf in the pan for about 5 minutes before cooling on a rack.

Nutritions *(Per serving):*

Calories: 153 kcal
Fat: 5.9 g

Carbohydrates: 24.5 g
Protein: 3.3 g

189. GLUTEN-FREE PULL-APART ROLLS

PREPARATION: 5 MIN   **COOKING:** 2 H   **SERVES:** 9

INGREDIENTS

- 1 cup warm water
- 2 tablespoons butter, unsalted
- 1 egg, room temperature
- 1 teaspoon apple cider vinegar
- 2 3/4 cups gluten-free almond-blend flour
- 1 1/2 teaspoons xanthan gum
- 1/4 cup sugar
- 1 teaspoon salt
- 2 teaspoons active dry yeast

DIRECTIONS

1. Add wet ingredients to the bread maker pan.
2. Mix dry ingredients except for yeast, and put in a pan.
3. Make a well in the middle of the dry ingredients and add the yeast.
4. Select the Dough cycle and press Start.
5. Spray an 8-inch round cake pan with non-stick cooking spray.
6. When the Dough cycle is over, roll the dough out into 9 balls, place in a cake pan, and baste each with warm water.
7. Cover with a towel and let rise in a warm place for 1 hour.
8. Preheat oven to 400°F.
9. Bake for 26 to 28 minutes; until golden brown.
10. Brush with butter and serve.

Nutritions *(Per serving):*

Calories: 568 kcal
Fat: 10.5 g

Carbohydrates: 116.3 g
Protein: 8.6 g

190. CLASSIC GLUTEN-FREE BREAD

PREPARATION: 5 MIN   **COOKING:** 1 H 10 MIN   **SERVES:** 12

INGREDIENTS

- 1/2 cup butter, melted
- 3 tbsp coconut oil, melted
- 6 eggs
- 2/3 cup sesame seed flour
- 1/3 cup coconut flour
- 2 tsp baking powder
- 1 tsp psyllium husks
- 1/2 tsp xanthan gum
- 1/2 tsp salt

DIRECTIONS

1. Pour in eggs, melted butter, and melted coconut oil into your bread machine pan.
2. Add the remaining ingredients to the bread machine pan.
3. Set bread machine to gluten-free.
4. When the bread is baked, remove the bread machine pan from the bread machine.
5. Let cool before transferring to a cooling rack.
6. You can store your bread for up to 3 days.

Nutritions *(Per serving):*

Calories: 146 kcal
Carbohydrates: 1.2 g

Protein: 3.5 g
Fat: 14 g

191. GLUTEN-FREE CHOCOLATE ZUCCHINI BREAD

PREPARATION: 5 MIN **COOKING:** 1 H 20 MIN **SERVES:** 12

INGREDIENTS

- 1 ½ cups coconut flour
- ¼ cup unsweetened cocoa powder
- ½ cup erythritol
- ½ tsp cinnamon
- 1 tsp baking soda
- 1 tsp baking powder
- ¼ tsp salt
- ¼ cup coconut oil, melted
- 4 eggs
- 1 tsp vanilla
- 2 cups zucchini, shredded

DIRECTIONS

1. Shred zucchini and strain excess water with paper towels.
2. Lightly beat eggs with coconut oil, then add to bread machine pan.
3. Add the remaining ingredients to the pan.
4. Set bread machine to gluten-free.
5. When the bread is baked, remove the bread machine pan from the bread machine.
6. Let cool before transferring to a cooling rack.
7. You can store your bread for up to 5 days.

Nutritions *(Per serving):*

Calories: 185 kcal
Carbohydrates: 6 g

Protein: 5 g
Fat: 17 g

192. NOT YOUR EVERYDAY BREAD

PREPARATION: 5 MIN | **COOKING:** 30 MIN | **SERVES:** 12

INGREDIENTS

- 2 tsp active dry yeast
- 2 tbsp inulin
- ½ cup warm water
- ¾ cup almond flour
- ¼ cup golden flaxseed, ground
- 2 tbsp whey protein isolate
- 2 tbsp psyllium husk finely ground
- 2 tsp xanthan gum
- 2 tsp baking powder
- 1 tsp salt
- ¼ tsp cream of tartar
- ¼ tsp ginger, ground
- 1 egg
- 3 egg whites
- 2 tbsp ghee
- 1 tbsp apple cider vinegar
- ¼ cup sour cream

DIRECTIONS

1. Pour wet ingredients into bread machine pan.
2. Add dry ingredients, with the yeast on top.
3. Set bread machine to basic bread setting.
4. When the bread is baked, remove the bread machine pan from the bread machine.
5. Let cool before transferring to a cooling rack.
6. You can store your bread for up to 5 days.

Nutritions *(Per serving):*

Calories: 175 kcal
Carbohydrates: 6 g

Protein: 5 g
Fat: 14 g

193. BANANA CAKE LOAF

PREPARATION: 5 MIN   **COOKING:** 40 MIN   **SERVES:** 12

INGREDIENTS

- 1 ½ cups almond flour
- 1 tsp baking powder
- ½ cup butter
- 1 ½ cups erythritol
- 2 eggs
- 2 bananas, extra ripe, mashed
- 2 tsp whole almond milk

DIRECTIONS

1. Mix butter, eggs, and almond milk together in a mixing bowl.
2. Mash bananas with a fork and add in the mashed bananas.
3. Mix all dry ingredients in a separate small bowl.
4. Slowly combine dry ingredients with wet ingredients.
5. Pour mixture into bread machine pan.
6. Set bread machine for bake.
7. When the cake is made, remove it from the bread machine and transfer it to a cooling rack.
8. Allow to cool completely before serving.
9. You can store your banana cake loaf bread for up to 5 days in the refrigerator.

Nutritions *(Per serving):*

Calories: 168 kcal
Carbohydrates: 7 g

Protein: 5 g
Fat: 14 g

194. ALMOND BUTTER BROWNIES

PREPARATION: 5 MIN | **COOKING:** 10 MIN | **SERVES:** 14

INGREDIENTS

- 1 cup almond butter
- 2 tbsp cocoa powder, unsweetened
- ½ cup erythritol
- ¼ cup dark chocolate chips, sugar-free
- 1 egg
- 3 tbsp almond milk, unsweetened

DIRECTIONS

1. Beat egg and almond butter together in a mixing bowl.
2. Add in erythritol and cocoa powder.
3. If the mixture is too crumbly or dry, add in almond milk until you have a smooth consistency.
4. Fold in dark chocolate chips.
5. Pour mixture into bread machine pan.
6. Set bread machine to bake.
7. When done, remove from bread machine and transfer to a cooling rack.
8. Cool completely before serving. You can store it for up to 5 days in the refrigerator.

Nutritions *(Per serving):*

Calories: 141 kcal
Carbohydrates: 3 g

Protein: 5 g
Fat: 12 g

195. ALMOND BUTTER BREAD

PREPARATION: 5 MIN | **COOKING:** 40 MIN | **SERVES:** 8

INGREDIENTS

- 1 cup coconut almond butter, creamy
- 3 eggs
- ½ tsp baking soda
- 1 tbsp apple cider vinegar

DIRECTIONS

1. Combine all ingredients in a food processor.
2. When the mixture is smooth, transfer to bread machine baking pan.
3. Set bread machine to bake.
4. When done baking, remove from the pan from your bread machine.
5. Allow cooling completely before slicing.
6. You can store it for up to 5 days in the refrigerator.

Nutritions *(Per serving):*

Calories: 175 kcal
Carbohydrates: 6 g

Protein: 5 g
Fat: 14 g

196. GLUTEN-FREE ALMOND BREAD

PREPARATION: 15 MIN   **COOKING:** 45 MIN   **SERVES:** 12

INGREDIENTS

- 2 cups almond flour, blanched
- ½ cup butter, melted
- 7 eggs
- 2 tbsp. avocado oil
- ½ tsp. xanthan gum
- ½ tsp. baking powder
- ½ tsp. salt

DIRECTIONS

1. Prepare bread machine loaf pan greasing it with cooking spray.
2. In a bowl, mix dry ingredients until well combined.
3. In another bowl, whisk eggs for 3 minutes or until they reach a creamy consistency.
4. Following the instructions on your machine's manual, mix the dry ingredients into the wet ingredients and pour in the bread machine loaf pan, taking care to follow how to mix in the baking powder.
5. Put the bread pan in the machine, select the basic bread setting, or gluten-free program, if available. Press start once you have closed the machine's lid.
6. When the bread is ready, using oven mitts, remove the bread pan from the machine.
7. Let it cool before slicing.
8. Cool, slice, and serve.

Nutritions *(Per serving):*

Calories: 247 kcal
Fat: 22.8 g

Carbohydrates: 4.9 g
Protein: 7.7 g

197. KETO ALMOND BREAD

PREPARATION: 10 MIN   **COOKING:** 30 MIN   **SERVES:** 4

INGREDIENTS

- 3 cups all-purpose flour
- 2 tsp crushed dried rosemary
- 1/2 tsp garlic powder
- 1/2 tsp ground thyme
- 3 tbsp olive oil
- 1 1/2 tsp salt
- 3 tbsp white sugar
- 2 1/2 tsp active dry yeast
- 1 cup warm water

DIRECTIONS

1. In a bowl, beat the cream of tartar and egg whites until soft peaks form.
2. Keep the mix on the side.
3. In a food processor, mix almond flour, salt, baking powder, egg yolks, and butter.
4. Add 1/3 cup egg whites to the food processor and pulse until combined.
5. Add rest of the egg whites and mix until combined.
6. Pour mixture into bread machine pan.
7. Set bread Basic program and start.
8. When baking is complete, remove from bread machine and transfer to a cooling rack.
9. When it is cool, slice, and serve.

Nutritions *(Per serving):*

Calories: 271 kcal
Fat: 22 g

Carbohydrates: 6 g
Protein: 5 g

198. CARROT CAKE

PREPARATION: 5 MIN   **COOKING:** 50 MIN   **SERVES:** 12

INGREDIENTS

- ½ cup erythritol
- ½ cup butter
- ½ tbsp vanilla extract
- 1 ¾ cups almond flour
- 1 ½ tsp baking powder
- 1 ½ tsp cinnamon
- ¼ tsp sea salt
- 1 ½ cup carrots, grated
- 1 cup pecans, chopped

DIRECTIONS

1. Grate carrots and place them in a food processor.
2. Add in the rest of the ingredients, except the pecans, and process until well incorporated.
3. Fold in pecans.
4. Pour mixture into bread machine pan.
5. Set bread machine to bake.
6. When baking is complete, remove from the bread machine and transfer to a cooling rack.
7. Allow to cool completely before slicing. (You can also top with a sugar-free cream cheese frosting, see recipe below).
8. You can store it for up to 5 days in the refrigerator.

Nutritions *(Per serving):*

Calories: 350 kcal
Carbohydrates: 8 g

Protein: 7 g
Fat: 34 g

199. SEEDED LOAF

| **PREPARATION:** 5 MIN | **COOKING:** 1-3 H | **SERVES:** 4 |

INGREDIENTS

- 7 eggs
- 1 cup almond flour
- ½ cup butter
- 2 tbsp olive oil
- 2 tbsp chia seeds
- 2 tbsp sesame seeds
- 1 tsp baking soda
- ½ tsp xanthan gum
- ¼ tsp salt

DIRECTIONS

1. Add eggs and butter to the bread machine pan.
2. Top with all other ingredients.
3. Set bread machine to the gluten-free setting.
4. Once done, remove from bread machine and transfer to a cooling rack.
5. This bread can be stored in the fridge for up to 5 days or 3 weeks in the freezer.

Nutritions *(Per serving):*

Calories: 190 kcal
Carbohydrates: 8 g
Fats: 18 g

Protein: 18 g

200. SIMPLE KETO BREAD

| **PREPARATION:** 3 MIN | **COOKING:** 1-3 H | **SERVES:** 8 |

INGREDIENTS

- 3 cups almond flour
- 2 tbsp inulin
- 1 tbsp whole milk
- ½ tsp salt
- 2 tsp active yeast
- 1 ¼ cups warm water
- 1 tbsp olive oil

Nutritions *(Per serving):*

Calories: 85 kcal
Carbohydrates: 4 g
Fats: 7 g
Protein: 3 g

DIRECTIONS

1. In a bowl, combine all the dry ingredients except for the yeast.
2. In the bread machine pan, add all wet ingredients.
3. Add all of your dry ingredients from the small mixing bowl to the bread machine pan. Top with the yeast.
4. Set the bread machine to the basic bread setting.
5. When the bread is baked, remove the bread machine pan from the bread machine.
6. Let cool before transferring to a cooling rack.
7. The bread can be stored for up to 5 days on the counter and 3 months in the freezer.

201. CLASSIC KETO BREAD

PREPARATION: 5 MIN   **COOKING:** 1-3 H   **SERVES:** 10

INGREDIENTS

- 7 eggs
- ½ cup ghee
- 2 cups almond flour
- 1 tbsp baking powder
- ¼ tsp salt

DIRECTIONS

1. Pour eggs and ghee into the bread machine pan.
2. Add remaining ingredients.
3. Set bread machine to a quick setting.
4. Let the bread machine complete its cycle.
5. When the bread is baked, remove the bread machine pan from the bread machine.
6. Let cool before transferring to a cooling rack.
7. The bread can be stored for up to 4 days on the counter and up to 3 months in the freezer.

Nutritions *(Per serving):*

Calories: 167 kcal   Fats: 16 g
Carbohydrates: 2 g   Protein: 5 g

TABLE OF CONTENTS

CPSIA information can be obtained
at www.ICGtesting.com
Printed in the USA
BVHW061110131221
623913BV00003B/309